Becoming a Woman of Value

How to Thrive in Life and Love

SANDY WEINER

Women's Empowerment and Dating Coach

Cover design by: Sandy Weiner

ISBN: 9798642255506

Dedicated to my two amazing daughters, Rebecca and Sara.

And to my two delicious granddaughters, Ora and Lielle.

You make a difference in my life and in every life you touch. May you continue to grow as true women of value.

I love you so much!

Table of Contents

Introduction

I f you've ever played small to make others comfortable, stayed quiet when you had something important to say, or stayed in a bad relationship or job for too long, because you didn't think you could do better, this book is for you.

I wrote it because I spent most of my life hiding who I really was. I didn't believe in my full potential, and I was convinced my life was as good as it could be. I stayed in an unhealthy marriage for 23 years. I believed it was virtuous to try and keep my family together—no matter what. My husband and I disagreed on just about everything, from how to raise our four children, to where to live, how to practice religion, what to eat, and how to communicate. For most of our marriage, we were not a team, the passion was missing, and we had very little in common.

Why did I stay? Divorce felt like failure, and I didn't want my kids to be the victims of a split household. Growing up in a high conflict home, my parents finally divorced when I was 29, the year I got married. I do believe my parents did the best they could, but I never wanted to put my kids through the pain I experienced as a child.

That's why I married a man who seemed to be a great candidate for father and husband—on paper. When we met, he was funny and attentive, kind and caring, and I thought we shared similar values and religious beliefs. His parents seemed to have a solid marriage, which I believed was a good predictor for our future. What could possibly go wrong?

Turns out—just about everything. From the outside, my life looked impressive. My husband had a very cool career as a professional comedian. He was the star and creator of a popular children's television show, and he was well-respected in the comedy world. We wrote comedy together, and I helped direct, edit, and design. We were kinda famous. I enjoyed working with him and stretching my creative talents.

I also had my own part-time business as an artist—painting furniture, murals, and creating ceramic works of art. Plus, I was the primary caretaker of our kids. I did it all—without outside support. I made all the doctor's appointments and took care of the kids and house. I was depleted, but I thought this was my lot in life. So I soldiered on…

While It was exciting working on a national TV show, and I loved raising my kids and working in a creative field, I often felt like I was sleep-walking through life. I was overworked, but my husband told me we couldn't afford help. I was exhausted, but, I'm not a quitter. So I kept on doing what I needed to do to survive. I often felt like I was an actor in a play, bending into a pretzel to make others happy.

Deep down, I knew that our marriage was beyond repair. But, I don't give up easily, and I wanted our marriage to work. So, I kept on trying to get through to him, to work things out. And he kept dismissing me. I felt stifled, small, and silenced. After 23 years, I had enough. The price I paid for keeping the peace had become too high, and I mustered up the courage to leave. I didn't divorce him because I fell in love with another man. I didn't leave because I was financially secure. I actually had no idea how I'd support myself or if I'd ever find true love.

I left to save myself.

Slowly, I began to change almost everything about my life. I became a solo homeowner for the first time, which was both terrifying and empowering. I started a new career as a life coach;

the certification program began the day I moved into my new home. In spite of all these major life changes, I was happier than I'd been in years.

From the day my marriage ended, I was on a journey. I didn't know it yet, but I was learning to become a woman of value, to embrace the gifts I was born with, to honor and love myself first. I had spent a lifetime putting everyone's needs before mine. It was time to prioritize my own needs and passions.

We're all born with natural talents and gifts, and many of us spend our lives covering them up.

We add layer upon layer of guards, fears, and doubts. We want to fit in, so we suppress who we are. We stop listening to our brilliant intuition, and we make poor choices in jobs, friends, and lovers. Eventually, many of us marry or enter into long-term relationships with people who don't value us.

We attract people into our lives in direct measure to our self-worth. If you don't love and value yourself, how can you expect others to love you?

Once I became a woman of value, I wanted to help other women value themselves more. My mission is to help women embrace their inner and outer beauty, wisdom, and talents, to know and communicate their worth, so they can live their best life.

This book is divided into what I call the 3 PILLARS OF CORE CONFIDENCE™.

1. **PILLAR I: SHOW UP.** In the first pillar, you'll fall in love with who you are today, because if you don't honor and value yourself, you won't be valued by others. You'll uncover limiting beliefs and replace them with empowering statements. And you'll rewire your brain in positive ways through daily practices.

2. **PILLAR II: STAND UP.** In the second pillar, you'll uncover your core values and what they stand for. You'll identify your standards and how you want to be treated by coworkers, romantic partners, and everyone else. You'll discover how to set clear boundaries and walk away from toxic relationships.

3. **PILLAR III: SPEAK UP.** In the final pillar, you'll learn how to communicate effectively, especially when stakes are high and you're feeling most vulnerable. Communication is a skill few people master. That's why I spent over a decade studying and teaching how to communicate with clarity and grace. I teach what I practice myself.

When you live as a woman of value, you will reap the benefits in all areas of your life.

You'll earn more respect at work, and you'll probably earn more money, because you will believe in and convey your worth. And you'll be surrounded by people who love and cherish you for who you are.

I hope you enjoy reading and practicing the exercises in *Becoming a Woman of Value*. Each step will bring you closer to living a life you love!

Sandy Weiner

Certified Life, Love, and Women's Empowerment Coach

https://thewomanofvalue.com

https://lastfirstdate.com

PILLAR I: SHOW UP

"Vulnerability is about showing up and being seen.

It's tough to do that when we're terrified about what people might see or think."

Brené Brown

Step 1: Love Yourself First

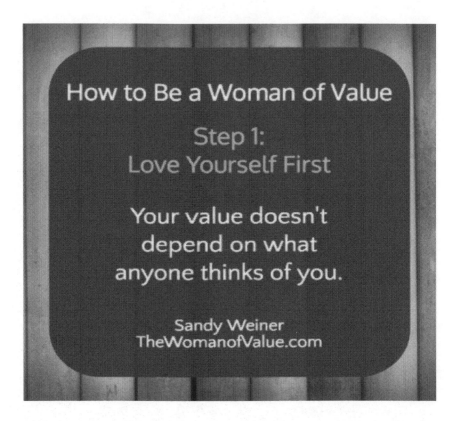

Love yourself first? The first time I heard about the importance of self-love, I didn't get it. It felt selfish to me. We're living in the "me, me, me" generation of selfies and constant posting on social media. Our society seems to be saturated with self-centered people. So, what does it mean to focus on self-love first?

In spite of all the selfies and naval gazing, so many of us lack self-love and self-worth. Why? It usually starts with our family of origin. Perhaps you were raised to be seen and not heard. Or you were valued for what you DID rather than who you WERE. Most of us were taught to be humble. The messages we heard at home sounded like, "Don't talk about yourself—that's immodest." "Be nice to others. Take care of your own needs after everyone else is happy." The result? Poor self-esteem.

I love this quote by John Lennon, which sums up the importance of self-love.

"There are two basic motivating forces: fear and love.

When we are afraid, we pull back from life.

When we are in love, we open to all that life has to offer with passion, excitement, and acceptance.

We need to learn to love ourselves first, in all our glory and our imperfections.

If we cannot love ourselves, we cannot fully open to our ability to love others or our potential to create.

Evolution and all hopes for a better world rest in the fearlessness and open-hearted vision of people who embrace life."

- John Lennon

What is self-love?

The self-love I'm referring to is about increasing your self-worth. It's about believing in yourself. It's about honoring your needs and feelings. It's about self-care, whatever that looks like to you. Maybe it's about finding your passion and following your bliss, instead of following someone else's vision of what you 'should' be doing with your life. It's about taking care of your body, mind, and spirit so that you're always striving to live your best life.

It's also about self-compassion. It's about forgiving yourself for your mistakes and imperfections. It's about falling in love with those imperfections and learning from the mistakes you might have made. If you don't love yourself first, you can't receive the love that is your birthright. You can't give from an openhearted place. You'll always be running on empty and you'll become depleted.

Have you ever been with someone who parses out love in tiny bits and pieces, each one so precious they're afraid to let go? Those people aren't filled with abundant love. Their love is scarce. They believe, "If I give it away, I'll lose a part of myself." I used to feel that way before I loved myself more. After my divorce, I started to pay attention to my needs and desires. I knew I was in charge of creating my life exactly as I wanted it, and I set out to find what made me happy, what brought me joy and love.

I knew that in order to attract my last first date, I'd have to fall in love with myself first. I have found work that fills me up, friends that feed my soul, and a life that fills me with more love than I ever imagined. Do you love yourself first? What will you do today to love yourself a little bit more?

Exercise to Create a Love Mantra

A love mantra is a positive affirmation to help you fall more in love with yourself. You repeat it every morning and night. It's to help you believe deep in your bones that you are lovable.

Here are some examples of love mantras:

"I AM CAPABLE OF ABUNDANT LOVE AND JOY."

"I GIVE AND RECEIVE EXTRAORDINARY LOVE."

"I STAY TRUE TO WHO I AM AT ALL TIMES. THE RIGHT PEOPLE WILL LOVE ME AS I AM."

Now, create your love mantra. It should be positive, optimistic, with room for the BIG love you deserve.

Step 2: Create a Life that Energizes You and Fills You Up

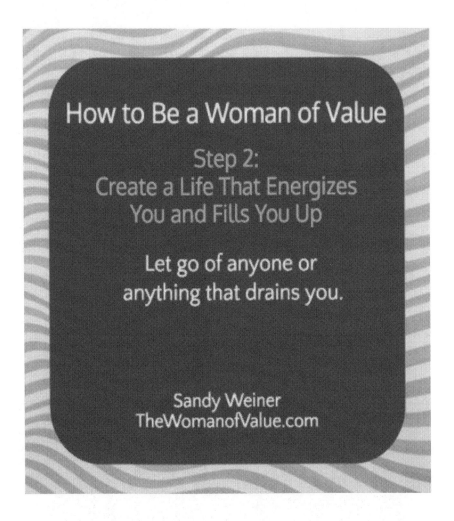

Do you love your life? Are your relationships draining or supportive? At the end of my marriage, I realized that many parts of my life were out of alignment, including my work and some of my friendships. Through the inner work I did with my coaches and therapists, I began to create a life I loved. When you live an inspired life, you inspire others. And you attract in relationships with people who add more sparks and light to your life.

Tired of living a life that's out of alignment? Reinvent your life.

After 25 years in the Corporate world, AnYes van Rhijn set up her own business as a life and business reinvention mentor. Having successfully reinvented herself three times (some call her "the Queen of reinvention"), she has become an expert in helping women who are at a crossroads, whatever the reason and whatever their age, to step into the driver seat of their life, and reinvent it! By connecting the dots between who they really are and what is important to them they can finally create a business and life that support each other. In my interview with AnYes, we spoke about how she reinvented herself and what she advises if you want to reinvent your life.

It's Never Too Late to Reinvent Your Life!

What are your beliefs in terms of reinventing your life?

We live in a world where it's rare that you stay in one career or business. We need to evolve if we want to survive. My major belief is that our choices our ruled by fear. You can begin to realize that most fears are not real. You then begin to make conscious choices, which dictate where you are in life. Then you're in the driver's seat.

9 years ago, I left the corporate world after 25 years. I had that nagging feeling that something was missing. I decided to step into my fear and start my own business. After 6-7 years, I discovered I was still being ruled by fear. I was afraid of financial insecurity and was still working only with the corporate world. I didn't like it. I was a sub-contractor making 6 figures, but almost went bankrupt because the companies I worked for lost big clients. I lost 70% of

my income. I rose up from my ashes, and two years ago, something happened in my personal life. I decided to leave a toxic relationship. It left me completely broke. I moved in with my sister.

Instead of looking at my situation as a victim, I looked at my role. I became conscious that there was a recurring pattern. I took charge. Looked inside and identified why I had landed in that situation. It became an amazing opportunity to reconsider my life choices.

I love how you focused on taking responsibility for your choices in life, and didn't remain a victim. Can you tell us how you healed?

It's so much easier to blame others than to look within. If you do look within and start to see how responsible you are for everything that happens in your life, you can change things. I had a healing process. It wasn't easy. I started to identify fear. That's how I was able to make a choice that was in alignment with me. I love working with women who want to leave the corporate world, or small business owners to connect the dots of all the parts of who they are so it's in alignment with their work.

What do you see as the biggest challenge that women are facing when it comes to making things happen for them?

Like me, many women leave the corporate world and don't know how to run a business or forget to take care of themselves. Something has to happen if they don't want to lose themselves in the process. The program I've developed helps women reinvent themselves to have the life they want, their version of success. They are able to set up their business environment and be in alignment with themselves.

You need clarity about what you want to achieve, and you need to take care of yourself first. Work in your business and ON your business. That's why my approach is holistic. A recent client said I have a "rare capacity to move with grace and ease between my left and right brain". [I think creatively, but know how to set up systems that work to help you succeed.]

Exercise for Reinventing Your Life

1. Don't let anyone tell you your dream is impossible.

2. You need to be extremely clear about who you are and what's important to you.

3. Constantly evaluate if your values and needs are being met and respected.

4. No one will ever succeed if you don't take a certain amount of risk.

5. Success doesn't happen overnight. You will sometimes move forward, sometimes move backwards.

6. Know your end goal. The journey will never be a straight line. You will adapt along the way.

Step 3: Be Playful

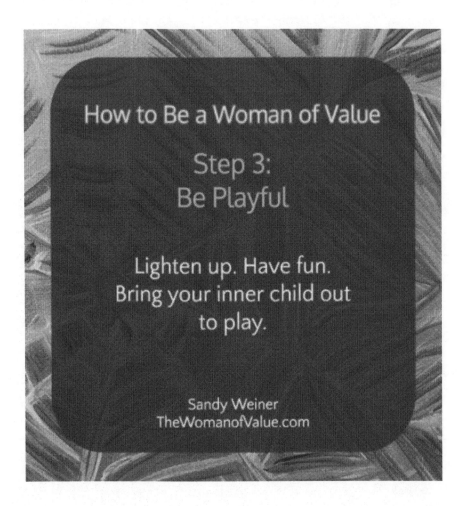

How to Be a Woman of Value

Step 3:
Be Playful

Lighten up. Have fun.
Bring your inner child out
to play.

Sandy Weiner
TheWomanofValue.com

As we reach our thirties, forties, and beyond, we often forget to play. We are so busy 'adulting' and being responsible for ourselves and our families, we put play and fun on the back burner. I think that's a big mistake. Without play, adventure, fun, and occasional silliness, we lose our spark. Life is best lived with gusto, and when you play, you let go. It's an amazing feeling!

My podcast guests, Drs. Rob + Janelle Alex, experts in relationship and intimacy dynamics, are mentoring couples around the globe. As best selling authors of the Mission Date Night Adventure series and cohosts of the Mission Date Night podcast, they help couples rediscover play, fun, and adventure. They believe married couples should continue to date and improve their lovemaking throughout their relationship. They're intent on obliterating long-standing relationships myths.

Following are loosely transcribed highlights of our interview, How to Keep the Spark Alive in a Long-Term Relationship.

Why do you believe couples need adventure in their relationships?

We need it in our life in general. When you have it in your relationship, it keeps things as fresh as it was during the courtship phase. It's easy to lose the connection and playfulness that helps a relationship stay strong. Laughter is the best medicine. It keeps romance, desire, passion and desire readily available and deepens the relationship all the time.

Once couples really get to know each other how can they feel mysterious and intriguing?

Do different things – get out of your rut. You can go on Mission Date Night adventures. You can do a Google search for date night ideas. Step a little bit out of your comfort zone together. It's amazing how your connection grows when you do something out of your comfort zone and experience it together.

If it's way out of your comfort zone, think about it before discounting it. It could lead to a great conversation about what types of things you'd like to try together. Create a bucket list. Set levels – a little or a lot out of the comfort zone. You might try going to a different type of restaurant and trying new foods together. You can even get dressed up, take on the persona of a

15

different woman, and meet your significant other at a bar for some excitement.

Do you believe that date nights should always lead to sex (lovemaking)?

Date night doesn't always have to lead to sex. And get your mind out of "sex is always intercourse". Foreplay begins in the morning when you wake up, the kiss goodbye, the texts and phone calls throughout the day. There's so much excitement that is sexual that doesn't even involve touching. There is so much energy that flows between the two of you.

Sex doesn't only have to be/shouldn't be goal-oriented. It's whatever you need in your relationship to stay close. Cuddle time can be just that. Communicate through talk and touch. It's so much more than just sex.

How can you manage your expectations in a long-term relationship?

Your expectations change and grow over time because YOU both change and grow over time. Your relationship shouldn't be goal-oriented either. There is no finish line when you meet that special person. It's a journey filled with peaks and valleys. Enjoy the journey together!

Exercise for Adding More Play and Fun Into Your Life

1. Make a list of 20 fun things you can do by yourself and with others.

2. Every day for the next week, add something fun to your day.

3. Journal daily about how you felt when you engaged in play and fun.

4. Now that you've seen the benefits, make fun a daily practice from now on.

Step 4: Love Your Body

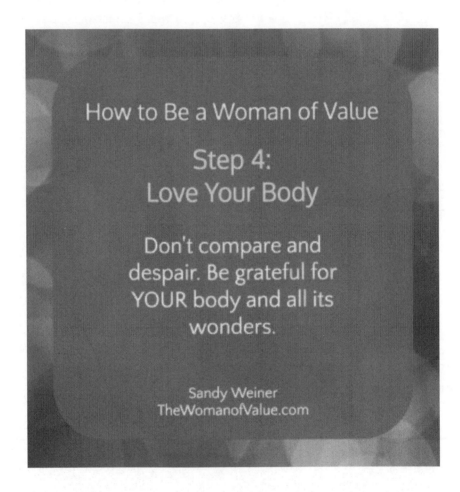

How to Be a Woman of Value

Step 4:
Love Your Body

Don't compare and despair. Be grateful for YOUR body and all its wonders.

Sandy Weiner
TheWomanofValue.com

Have you ever struggled with body image? Most of us have. Whether you are overweight, underweight, or just the right weight, it seems that most of us look for what's wrong with our bodies, not what's right.

My body story

I was thin most of my life. In fact, in my teens, I was so thin, my Aunt Elsie would say, "You're too skinny. You need to eat more." And then she'd shove a plate of Drake's Yankee Doodle pastries at me. Or it could be any creme-filled chocolatey gooey cake that came out of a box. This was heaven to me and my siblings. I would eat those cakes and never gain weight. In fact, I would eat an entire loaf of bread with butter in one sitting, and I remained as thin as ever. Did I love my body back then? No. I felt I was too tall and too thin.

By seventh grade, I was embarrassed that I still didn't get my period and my chest was flat as a board. So what did I do? I stuffed by bra with stockings. Yep, stockings. It was quite a task to get it right, too. I had to shape them into a boob-like blob to fill the bra up every single day. My new fake boobs made me feel more womanly. But, they also complicated my life. I couldn't get undressed in front of friends at sleepovers. And as I got older, I was scared that a guy would want to feel me up. It would have been mortifying to have a guy find out they were fake. I thought men wouldn't like me as much if I had small boobs.

By senior year, I said to myself, "Enough with the boob stuffing!" I took the stockings out. Then I got rid of the bras altogether! I had perky small breasts, and I didn't need a bra for support. I went from one extreme to the other, and I loved my newfound freedom. Did I love my body? Not really. I was still critical of my cellulite. I wanted a flatter belly, thinner thighs. I began to work out, biking all over town instead of driving.

When I was twenty-four, I moved to Manhattan, and for the next few years, I was in the best shape of my life. I walked four miles to work and back every day. In the evenings, I lifted weights and took exercise classes. I was flexible and strong. My arms were in amazing shape. Did I love my body? Not really. I thought it was okay, but I didn't appreciate the shape I was in. My self-esteem was moderate, but when it came to men, I didn't value myself enough.

Today, I am post-menopausal, and I've gained weight. My fast metabolism has slowed down. I have wrinkles, and my muscles are weaker. I sit most of the day for work. I walk about 45 minutes every day, and that's pretty much the only exercise I get. Do I love my body? I finally appreciate my body. I have so much gratitude for being able to walk and stretch and recover from injuries quickly. I am grateful for every day I have on this planet, every day that my body functions well. It's so important to be kind to yourself and your body, to love your unique style and your special brand of beauty. I didn't appreciate the body of my youth, but I do appreciate my body today.

How can you learn to appreciate your body more?

Work on loving yourself, all of you, cellulite, wrinkles, zits, scars, saggy parts, hairy parts, bumpy lumpy dumpy parts. All of it. Your hair, whether it's thick or thin, short or long, or not there at all. We buy beauty products to look younger and sexier. We inject botox and collagen, go for facials and chemical peels.

Here's what I have to say…

ENOUGH!

Let's do something about all this criticism of our bodies…

Exercise: The Inner Critic Diet©

This exercise is by Nina Manolson, MA, Psychology of Eating Teacher & Health Coach, at **NinaManolson.com**

The Inner Critic Diet©

Step #1:

AWARENESS

(day 1 & 2)

Notice the inner critic.

Listen carefully to what and how your "mean mirror voice" expresses herself.

Write down 5 things your critical voice says (ie. your belly's too big, your arms are too flappy, your hair is too thin – what

YOU specifically say to yourself).

Getting to know your inner critic/mean mirror voice allows you to differentiate her voice from your higher self/authentic voice.

Step #2:

SELF-COMPASSION

(day 3 & 4)

Interrupt the critic's voice with self-compassion and loving kindness.

Experiment with these two phrases to see what resonates best for you:

May I love myself completely, just the way I am.

May warmth and kindness fill my heart. May I love myself.

Step #3:

ZOOM OUT

(day 5 & 6)

imagine your eyes are like a camera lens than can zoom out to the whole of you - the whole of your physical self and the whole of your inner world.

Look in the mirror and zoom out to see **your specific brand of beauty**!

Step #4:

BE REALLY NICE & LET THE KINDNESS IN

(day 7)

Say nice things to yourself, eg. "I look nice today" or "that color looks really good on me."

Start flexing the be-nice-to-yourself muscle. Let in your kindness!

REPEAT IN ANY ORDER AND AT ALL TIMES!

Love your body more starting today. And please stop comparing yourself to anyone else. Be kind to yourself.

Step 5: Own Your Beauty

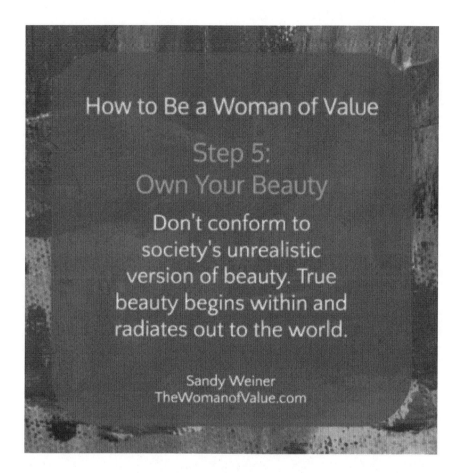

We are all beautiful in our own unique way. When do we start to forget?

When my first granddaughter was two-years old, she loved to walk around naked, with her adorable round belly hanging out in all its glory. She had rolls of fat on each arm and leg, which made her even more delicious to squeeze and hug. She had absolutely no problem asking for whatever she wanted. She could even be a little bossy sometimes. But, nobody seemed to mind. Because she was so darn cute. She was feisty and funny, curious and playful.

Here's how this plays out…

In about ten years (maybe sooner), she'll probably begin to lose confidence. She won't think she's pretty enough. She'll start hating her body. It will be so hard to witness. Unfortunately, this is the norm. Even if we grow up in a loving home with lots of positive support, we are influenced by our surroundings, our friends, and the media. We compare and despair. No matter your size, shape, or the color of your skin, most women don't think they're beautiful…even super models.

My beauty story:

My father would always tell me I was beautiful, but I didn't believe him. He was my dad, and dads are a little biased, right?

My parents' friends used to tell me I had beautiful skin, but I didn't believe them. I was young, and young people have naturally beautiful skin, right? One of my best friends in high school compared me to a super model at that time, and I couldn't see the similarities.

No matter who told me I was beautiful, I didn't believe them. I thought I was okay looking. Passable. Certainly not beautiful. And I carried that story with me most of my life.

What is beauty?

Many women have told me they don't feel they're as beautiful as other women in their town. If they can't compete in the dating scene, they'd rather remain single. I don't believe beauty is a one-size-fits-all standard. I also don't believe beauty is about flawless skin, youth, or a 'perfect' body.

Beauty begins on the inside with the way you feel about yourself. Not how others look or feel about YOU, but how you feel about YOU. One of the best ways to increase your confidence is by taking emotional risks. Apply for the job you thought was for someone much more experienced. Flirt with the cute guy at your gym. Leave a job you hate, and start your own business. Travel alone. What have you been scared to do? Do that!

What's your beauty story?

Were you told you were beautiful as a child? As an adult? By a significant other?

Were you told you were unattractive by friends, bullies, an ex-boyfriend or husband?

Here's what I know for sure now that I'm in my sixties: no one gets to decide how beautiful we are. That's our choice.

But, how do we begin to embrace our own brand of beauty? Beauty begins on the inside. With taking emotional risks as stated above. And most importantly, it is about a practice of kindness to your self, of self-compassion. This exercise will help you begin a practice of self-compassion.

Exercise: The Self-Compassionate Day

It's amazing how many of our decisions come from fear. You eat a certain way due to fear of gaining weight. You stay at a job you don't like because of fear of being broke. You stay in a relationship that's demeaning because you're afraid to be alone.

From the minute you wake up until the time you go to sleep, reframe everything you do as coming from a place of love, not fear.

For example, at breakfast, say to yourself:

1. I'm eating this food because I love my body and want to stay healthy.

Other options include:

* This brings me pleasure.

* This will give me energy.

* I take time to prepare my food, because I honor my body.

2. Notice what happens

Over time, you'll rewire your brain for love, not fear. Your ability to be kind to yourself will increase exponentially.

3. Other way to be kinder to yourself

You can also ask yourself, "What do I need now to be kinder to myself?" Is there a phrase that speaks to you in your particular situation, such as:

* I will give myself the compassion I need

* I will learn to accept myself as I am

* I will stop comparing myself to others

* I will be patient with myself as I grow and evolve into the fullest expression of myself

This practice can be used any time of day or night, and it will help you remember to bring forth self-compassion when you need it most. That is where your TRUE beauty stems from —within.

Step 6: Learn to RECEIVE graciously

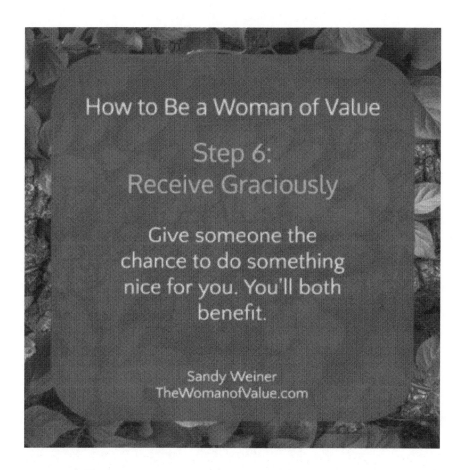

How easy is it for you receive? If you're like most women I know, you're a giver, but you're not comfortable taking. I want to stress the importance of receiving, especially in dating and relationships. Think about how good it feels for you to give. If you are not a 'receiver', you take away the pleasure of giving from your friend, colleague, date, or lover. Women are trained to give and give, often to depletion. That makes you an exhausted martyr, not a better person!

Women are built to receive

Mother nature had it right. Think about it this way. Women have vaginas. They are built to receive during sexual intercourse with a man. Men have penises, and they are built to give during sex. When women graciously receive from men, it makes men feel good about giving or providing, which is how he defines his masculinity.

To dive deeper into this topic, dating and relationship coach, Nicole DiRocco, founder of Dating with Grace, joined me on Last First Date Radio. Nicole understands the challenges facing women in the business world and how working in such an environment can influence how women approach dating and relationships. Knowing that it is being in your feminine grace that will attract the right man, Nicole supports smart, savvy professional women gain the know-how they need to date successfully. Nicole spoke about <u>How to Unleash Your Feminine Grace to Win His Love</u>. Following are loosely transcribed highlights of the show.

How to Unleash Your Feminine Grace to Win His Love

Why do you call yourself a recovering HR executive?

Recovering equals stopping a harmful behavior. I spent many years in the corporate world. Then, something happened that brought awareness to a harmful behavior. I was taking painting lessons, and my instructor wanted me to add more paint and more detail. I didn't want to add more paint, as I didn't want to mess it up. It was acrylic, and you can't really mess it up! But, each week, my instructor told me the same thing; add more detail and more paint. Then it hit me. When I don't feel comfortable, I procrastinate.

At the same time, I was in a coaching program, and I brought this up to my mentor. She asked, "Are you getting a grade in the painting class?" I said, "No". She said, "The highly competitive corporate world you came from made you always have to be the expert and in control. What would it be like if the painting class was just fun?" I went back to the class and added more paint and detail and it was so much better! Being in your feminine grace is about bringing that lightness and fun into your life.

What else does it mean to be in your feminine grace?

It's not about being submissive or giving up your power. When a woman is in her feminine grace, she gives power to herself and to her man. Most women are attracted to men who lead, men with character. Most strong leaders tend to care less about a certain body type and face. They place more value on a woman's behaviors and character. Feminine grace is the foundation by which a woman lives her life in order to be happy. She loves every aspect of being a woman. She doesn't need a man to be complete. She is happy to say she wants a man. She doesn't use her gender as an excuse for what doesn't work in her life. She's confident, takes responsibility for her actions. She likes and appreciates men.

How can a woman learn to trust and like men if she's had bad experiences throughout her life?

Every man is an individual, and you can't project onto a man due to bad past experiences. A woman in her feminine grace is present, not living in the past. She needs to dig deep within herself, and remove the barriers that are keeping her closed. It helps to have a coach assist with this type of deeper work.

How does she get into her feminine grace?

She practices extreme self-care, doing things that make her happy. For example, I declared that I wanted to have a joyful life and do things that bring me joy. That's why I took up painting and a wine class. I went on a food and wine excursion through Provence! One of my travel companions was a Holocaust survivor. I spent eight inspiring days with her. I created joy in my life.

When I do things that bring me joy, I attract joy. Then I can focus on who to attract into my life. Feminine grace means you attract love from the inside out. A man knows you're happy already, and wants to make you happier. Men are attuned to a woman who likes herself and places a priority on herself.

Why do you say that a woman needs to have a vision for the life she wants to create before she looks for a partner?

It's important to be crystal clear about what your core needs and values are. You need to know what kind of life you want to create before looking for a partner. You see if he'll fit into that life, not the other way around.

What do you mean by a man showing a woman who he is on a first date?

I've spent a lot of time in the people business, teaching how to be effective in communication. I've learned that men say what they mean from the get-go. Look for clues and step over nothing. But don't interrogate.

Here's an example:

I recently had a first date with someone I met online. I told him I don't like to text and prefer phone calls. We spoke on the phone, and he asked me to dinner near my home. A few hours after the phone call, he texted, "I know you don't like to text, but…" He was dismissing how I like to receive communication.

When we met, he was a gentleman. Ordered wine. He took the lead. I loved being in my feminine grace! He was intrigued by the fact that I'm a coach. He shared that he had a coach to help with an issue at work. Then, he kept referring to his ex. His profile said he was a widower. He said, "Oh no, I have to go in and correct that. I'm divorced after a long marriage. My ex-wife and I have a contentious relationship. She poisoned the kids against me. One of my kids doesn't talk to me."

I sensed this was a man who had resentment and unresolved conflict in his life, and I didn't want to date him again. I told him we were not a match and wished him the best in his search. Pay attention to your gut feelings about what a man reveals in those first conversations. You'll learn so much about his true character before you become clouded by attraction hormones.

Exercise: Practice Asking for Help

Every day for the next week, ask someone for help. Be specific about what kind of help you need. And tell the person why you chose them to help you. Graciously receive the help, and note what happens to you as you begin to ask for and receive more support.

Step 7: Be the LOVE you wish to find in the world

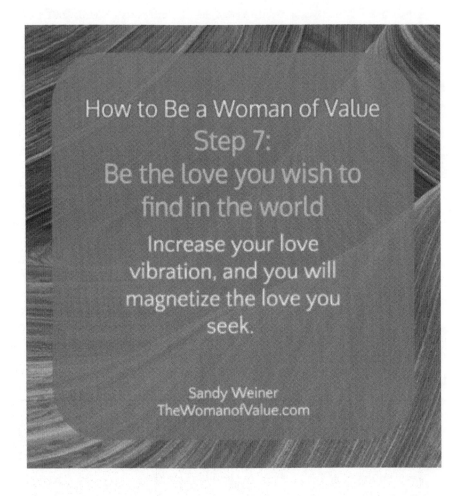

Mahatma Gandhi said, "Be the change that you wish to see in the world". My version is, "Be the love you wish to find in the world."

Whether you're searching for your last first date, or you're in a relationship that's stale or troubled, it's helpful to reflect on who you're being and what you're contributing to relationships. It requires an honest look at yourself, to see if you're the partner that your ideal partner is seeking.

Let's say you're seeking a partner who is kind. Is there an area in your life where you can increase kindness? You want a partner who is generous. Is there an area in your life where you could be more generous?

My client, Maureen, shared her transformation to become the LOVE she was seeking.

My Love Story, by Maureen

I divorced after a thirty-three year marriage and was ecstatic I could now be "me" again and was free to go in the direction of my heart. Within a year-and-a-half, I had begun online dating, and I eventually met a man I was sure was a good match for me. I found, however, that I would need to leave the relationship about every six weeks. I began having serious doubts about myself and since I had never been one to leave a commitment, I really didn't understand my own behavior. Why was I running away from what seemed like a great relationship?

I knew all the right words but couldn't express my feelings (or even identify them!) or make my actions match my words and feelings.

It seemed everything else in my life was wonderful...I loved my job, friends, activities...so why was this part of my life so hard and awkward? I wanted what he offered and yet, I couldn't accept it. I heard, "You're beautiful", "You're smart", "You make my life better" but just couldn't believe it. I couldn't figure out what was "wrong" with me, much less, how to fix it.

When he finally decided he could no longer take the "yoyo" relationship, he told me I needed some reflection time

and would be happy and complete when I figured out what I wanted.

After spending my winter break in full despondency mode, I began looking for information online, read every blog I could find, reviewed books, and watched online relationship instructional videos. I knew I needed a mentor, someone who had been through this and could see from the outside where I was in this journey.

The self-love journey begins...

Enter Sandy, a kind, compassionate, wise soul. After talking with her, I knew she was a great match for me. I jumped in wholeheartedly to push myself out of my box. Our weekly calls were a lifesaver for me and kept me sane and focused while I grew inside in fits, starts, and bursts. I was exposed to new ways of thinking, responding, new strategies, and books that opened my eyes.

I learned I had spent my life fixing, well, trying to fix, others and just wore my emotional self out because it's an impossible task! I focused on noticing my own triggers and practicing new responses. I've had so many "aha!" moments, I've stopped keeping track of them!

I began to trust myself, others, and the universe and to be open and accepting of others and events. My life began to change as I learned to identify my boundaries and how to negotiate and share feelings kindly but firmly with others. I now have a view of myself and life that I've never had before. I've always been a positive person, but mostly positively sure I could either fix or help everyone. Now, my life is so expansive, open, accepting, curious, and loving in the present moment, as virtually any situation that arises.

I created "confidence" cards from the new wisdom and carry them with me always. They give me gentle reminders of boundaries, attachment, trusting, accepting, values, authenticity, self-compassion, and expectations. It's like carrying a tiny Sandy with me! My "angel" keeps my gremlin in check and allows light in places that haven't seen light in decades. I've become myself but a bigger, grander version. I'm still opening up and growing and at times, it feels as though I barely have time in my day for a sad thought. I find myself smiling randomly and overcome with happiness and gratitude.

Since my coaching with Sandy, I've put to rest a relationship where I felt less than "me", gone on several fun and "interesting" first dates, and even bought a house!

I know I'm ready to move on and am creating the life that feels uplifting and authentic to me. I've learned to listen to advice and take what I need from it. I've shared with others parts of my journey and a number of friends are now on similar paths. They have also begun reaching out for help and we support each other in positive ways, instead of complaining and agreeing that our lives are a daily struggle.

My biggest "aha!" moment was when I actually was able to put into action the idea of not attaching to the outcome.

The house buying process can definitely promote attachment, but I was able to walk away from those I was outbid on or were out of my range. I knew in my heart that it would all work out and the attachment just wasn't there. I put the effort in, and the rest was out of my control.

I'm so excited to see what is next for me but don't have the feeling I need to grab at straws, or men, just to complete my life.

I now have the confidence to reach out to others, whether it be male, female, young, old, and share their sorrows and joys. It's easy for me to talk with strangers or dates without judging either myself or them. I'm not pining away for someone to rescue me from myself, but sharing myself with others. A light inside has been turned on and I'm sharing the real me with the world! Thank you, Sandy, for being who you are and giving your gifts to those in need!

UPDATE: Maureen is in the best relationship of her life. I believe she met her best partner, because she became the love she wished to find in the world.

Exercise to Be the Love to Attract in Love

* Make a list of all the traits you would like in your ideal partner.

* Now, take a look at that list and honestly assess whether you have each of those traits.

* For any trait that's either missing or or not fully realized, what's one small step you can take to improve in this area? Repeat with every trait until you feel that you're truly living the love you wish to find in the world.

Step 8: Be more vulnerable

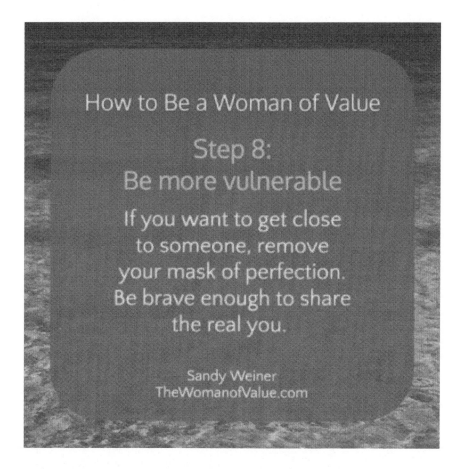

How to Be a Woman of Value

Step 8:
Be more vulnerable

If you want to get close
to someone, remove
your mask of perfection.
Be brave enough to share
the real you.

Sandy Weiner
TheWomanofValue.com

If you consistently guard your heart from pain, you will stay safe from heartache. You'll also guard your heart from love.

The secret to authentic deep relationships is vulnerability. When you express your feelings and needs, he will be more likely to express his. When you talk about your fears, you give him the space to speak about his. This chapter is brought to you by my friend, 'Stacy Beckwith'. Stacy used a pseudonym to protect the feelings of past partners and family members. I admire her integrity. Writers walk a fine line between sharing and over-sharing.

Stacy and I first met when she commented on one of my Huffington Post articles. We began to develop a friendship based on shared experiences—especially about divorce, relationships, and entrepreneurship. Over one weekend, one of our conversations helped her realize why she was never able to fall in love. Her experience was so profound, I asked her to share it with me in an article. Here it is.

Princess Built Herself a Fortress

by Stacy Beckwith

I have never been in love. There, I said it. I was married for almost 20 years and have been part of two, very serious, post-divorce relationships. I truly loved those men as people, enjoyed their company, and had lots of fun. But no, I did not romantically love them, even though I told them I did. I thought I was staying for security and my deep fear of being alone. But then, my friend Sandy Weiner shared her TEDx talk (about turning into a Tootsie Pop and guarding your heart in relationships so you won't get hurt).

I came to realize it was actually something very different. I was with these men because I was never going to love them, and *if I didn't fall in love with them, they could never hurt me*. My heart was perfectly protected in this fortress where there was no chance for love so no chance for pain…and I was utterly miserable.

As each relationship ended I was devastated I had allowed myself to stay when I was not in love. And then I vowed to really fall in love the next time. But rather than follow that plan, I walked into the next one knowing I would never love him either. I was living in a cycle of "I would rather build a relationship than a wall. Can you pass me another brick?"— Jarod Kintz, This Book Has No Title. When my last significant relationship ended, I knew I really needed to change. Next time around I was going to get it right. Look around and find a guy I could actually fall in love with and then love him with great abandon. I put my integrity in double check and vowed to mean what I say and say what I mean with those three little magic words.

And I promised to sit in the seat of vulnerability and accept the risk of being hurt.

I put myself out there and went on many many dates. And then it happened. I walked into a bar on a Wednesday night in early July to meet another online dating victim, took one look in his eyes and thought "oh crap, this guy is the real deal." It wasn't love at first sight, but there was a stirring, and I was scared to death. Online dating profiles were down within a week.

And as we have marched through these early dating days together, I have caught myself putting timeframes around moving forward, like "there is no way I can love him until three months have passed. Don't get too attached, it is too soon. What if my feelings are not reciprocated? My friends need to approve of him." I've been looking for red flags, scrutinizing his every move, spending way too much time thinking.

Princess has been building herself a different kind of fortress to house her heart. This one is filled with challenges and obstacles for the relationship to jump through before deemed worthy to receive the keys to the inner sanctuary. A moat to swim, dragons to slay, walls to scale. All done in the name of moving slowly, not rushing, not getting hurt. All ensuring I am not dating a Trojan Horse who is going to gain entrance and then unleash fury. Not feeling, just evaluating.

But in reality, you cannot intellectualize love and felt connection…the truth here is that I am falling, my heart is winning over my head. Rather than test the relationship to gain passage, the door is naturally starting to lower over the moat. My heart is ready to burst out. It is easy; he is everything that I want in a partner. A center core of integrity, a fantastic father, we have matched energy, trust has been firmly established, safety is felt. It is time to stop construction, stop protecting, and start to really live this gift I have been given.

Maybe it is time to put the fortress on the market, and instead move into a nice four bedroom colonial in suburbia with big open windows for this to breathe and a front door with two sets of keys —hey, wait a minute….we are house shopping?!?! Isn't it too soon??

Post Script: Three years later, 'Stacy' and her boyfriend did move into that nice four-bedroom house together. They're now happily married. She's in love, and her heart is out of the fortress. And she's never been happier.

Exercise to Un-guard Your Heart

Have you ever felt like Stacy? Have you guarded yourself from the possible pain of heartbreak, afraid to let go and let love in?

Journal about some of the ways you've guarded your heart in the past. Then, challenge yourself to get more vulnerable. On your next date, share a fear or a flaw you're working on. Journal about what happens when you do that. How did he respond?

Step 9: Love is your birthright

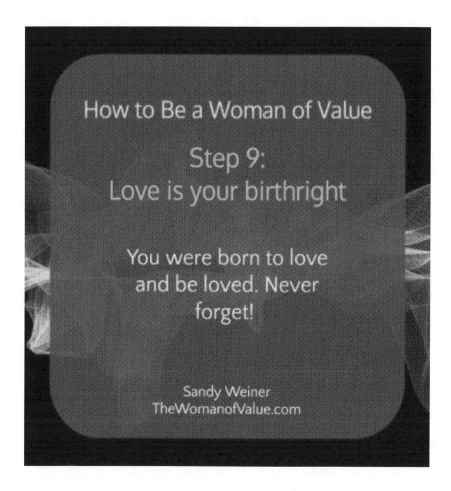

Love really is your birthright! You were born to love and be loved. You ARE love. So, why is it so hard for many of us to believe in our inherent lovability?

Maybe you grew up in a home where you had to DO something to be loved. You had to prove your worth by getting good grades or being the best gymnast or having the starring role in the school play. You were loved when you did something positive, and your parents rewarded you for that with a smile, a hug, or maybe just not yelling or punishing you.

This is very common, and it's a terrible paradigm for love. When you believe you have to DO to receive love, you don't believe enough in your worth. You don't believe you are enough without achieving and proving.

Why do our parents make us perform like monkeys in a circus? It's because many of them didn't receive love just for BEING. So, they passed it down to us. And we carry that limiting belief, that love is about DOING. And love only happens for a few select lucky people. The good news? You can break that stinking legacy. Here's how.

Heal your inner child.

In this interview with Dr. Margaret Paul, co-founder of Inner Bonding, we discuss the inner child and how you can heal and give yourself the love you didn't receive from your parents.

What is the 'inner child' and why is it so important to be in tune with yours?

Your inner child is your soul, essence, core self, and feeling self. When you get a feeling of anxiety or depression or anger, it's your inner child letting you know that you are abandoning yourself. In the part of our brains called the amygdala, our false beliefs get programmed. When our intention is to protect against pain with controlling behavior, we are operating from the wounded ego. Our inner child reacts to let you know that your wounded self is in charge and the inner child is abandoned. When you're creative and full of love, you're operating out of the loving adult self, or your higher self. You're connecting to your higher source which guides you.

What do you mean by self-abandonment and how does this affect relationships?

When you abandon yourself, you give your inner child away to another person, and you're upset that person doesn't give you what you need. Most people are in relationships to get something from another person. We can only share love when we practice self-love first. Then it can overflow. Getting love doesn't bring joy. The greatest joy is sharing love.

What are the six steps of Inner Bonding? [From The Six Steps of Inner Bonding Home Study Course]

Step One: Become mindful of your feelings. Decide that you want to take 100% responsibility for the ways in which you may be causing your own pain, and for creating your own peace and joy.

Step Two: Choose the intent to learn to love yourself and others. Making this choice opens your heart, allows Divine Love, in and moves you into your loving adult self.

Step Three: Choose to welcome, embrace and dialogue with your wounded self, exploring your thoughts/false beliefs and the resulting behaviors that may be causing your pain. Bring compassion to your core-Self feelings. Explore your gifts and what brings joy to your core Self.

Step Four: Dialogue with your spiritual Guidance, discovering the truth and loving action toward your self.

Step Five: Take the loving action learned in Step Four.

Step Six: Evaluate the effectiveness of your loving action.

Exercise: The Six Steps of Inner Bonding

These steps are a powerful roadmap to healing the false beliefs that may be keeping you limited in your personal life and at work.

Always remember that you are worthy of giving and especially receiving love.

Step 10: Forgive yourself and others

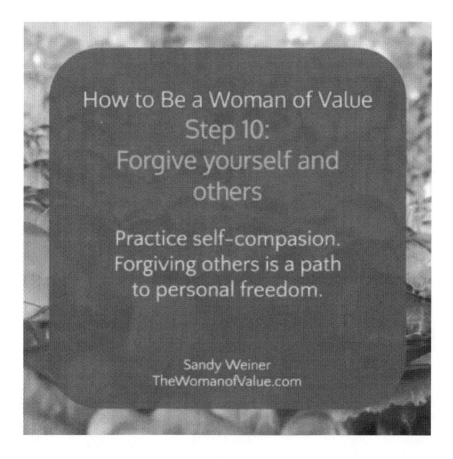

How to Be a Woman of Value
Step 10:
Forgive yourself and others

Practice self-compasion.
Forgiving others is a path
to personal freedom.

Sandy Weiner
TheWomanofValue.com

Some people do awful things. Things that are hurtful. Things that feel unforgivable. So, why should we forgive the people who hurt us? Because it's good for US. It's so we can release past pain and move on without carrying any bitterness or regret. When you hold onto anger at someone else, the only person who suffers is you. There is no virtue in staying angry, but there is incredible release in letting go.

This is not about *condoning* bad behavior. It's about forgiving (not forgetting). By doing this exercise, you'll be able to release painful experiences and memories, to clear the way for you to open your heart again.

Exercise for forgiving those who hurt you

1. Make a list of things you need to forgive in OTHERS

Write down any traumatic events or embarrassing moments from any period in your life.

Examples:

- Romantic relationships where you were hurt

- Bosses or colleagues who were mean in any way

- Friends who teased you or were unkind

- Strangers who were cruel, either in real life or on the web/social media

- Teachers who made you feel bad on a report card or test/paper, or publicly in front of the class

Write a sentence or two about each pain point. For example, "When my ex-husband walked away in the middle of an argument..." or "That time my teacher called me lazy in front of the class..."

2. Forgive and let go

Go through each item, and say out loud to yourself:

"You did the best you could with the tools you had."

"I let go of expecting you to be any different."

"I forgive you."

Exercise for forgiving those you hurt

1. Make a list of anything you want to forgive YOURSELF for

Examples:

- You beat yourself up for failing at something

- You were unkind to a friend

- You broke up with a man in a way you regret

- You gossiped behind someone's back

- You embarrassed someone or made someone cry (intentionally or not)

- You stole something, big or small

- You cheated on something

Write a sentence or two about each pain point. For example, "That time I was mean to the new girl in school..." or "When I copied my friend's paper in 8 grade..."

2. Forgive and let go

Go through each item, and say out loud to yourself:

"I did the best I could with the tools I had."

"I will do better next time."

"I forgive myself."

Why?

"I did the best I could with the tools I had" helps you bring compassion to yourself and the situation or person, and it releases you from feeling bitter or holding onto remorse.

"I will do better next time." Helps you focus on who you are NOW and stop beating yourself up about something you did in the past.

I forgive myself" begins to release any anger or resentment you might still be holding onto.

Check your list again in a few days

After a few days, go over each item on your list and see if there's any negative 'charge' or feeling still remaining. You might be surprised to find that you can't even remember some of the reasons why you were angry or resentful. If negative feelings remain, repeat the exercise until the embarrassment or anger you once felt begins to fall away.

Observe

With forgiveness and letting go, you'll feel much happier and lighter.

You'll be free of the negative energy and anger, which will open you up to new possibilities in life and love.

Over time, you'll stop thinking about the people you held onto with resentment for so long. You have given yourself a wonderful gift – freedom and lightness.

This forgiveness exercise can transform your life. Repeat as necessary.

PILLAR II: STAND UP

"Trust your own instincts, go inside, follow your heart. Right from the start, go ahead and stand up for what you believe in. As I've learned, that's the path to happiness."

Lesley Ann Warren

Step 11: Don't be a people pleaser

If you grew up in a dysfunctional home with an alcoholic or codependent parent or spouse, you're probably used to giving to others and ignoring your own needs.

You give and give, trying to make things better or get people to like you more. You give just a little bit more. And you don't ask for much in return. And the resentment builds, but you don't want to be MEAN…

Why do you give so much? Maybe you feel guilty saying no when someone asks for a favor. Or perhaps you don't even know what you need, you're so used to morphing into what others need of YOU. It's challenging for most people to identify and communicate what they need from others.

Perhaps you've asked for help, but when others didn't reciprocate, you surrendered in frustration and continued to do it all yourself. That's exhausting!

Maybe you woke up one day to the realization that you'd given up important bits of yourself in a relationship. You became resentful. When your partner/boss/friend failed to meet your needs, your resentment grew. Perhaps you assumed he or she didn't care enough about you to give back. You felt trapped in a bad relationship. You felt unvalued and undesired.

If you recognize yourself as a people-pleaser, the People Pleaser Cure is for you!

The People-Pleaser Cure: Four Steps to Create the Life and Love You Deserve

When you make your needs less important and only attend to others, you lose yourself. The antidote to people-pleasing is to turn your needs way up. You need to put yourself on top of your to-do list. You matter! *If you don't take care of yourself, no one will respect you.*

1. Stop neglecting your basic needs. Are you eating healthy food and getting exercise on a regular basis? Are you fulfilling your intellectual and emotional needs? Are you making time for activities that make you happy? Are you getting enough sleep? Figure out what needs you've been neglecting and make a list. Post it on the bathroom mirror, above your desk, or on your computer. Your needs matter. You want to remember that every day. And then…

2. Work on attending to one need a week. Take that list, and tackle one need a week. Taking baby steps will help you begin to put yourself at the top of your to-do list. Catch up on your sleep. Read that exciting new book. Go out with friends. Do whatever it is that you've been neglecting. But don't try to change everything at once or you'll burn out. One need a week should do the trick.

3. Stop saying 'yes' when you mean 'no'. When someone asks you for a favor and you have trouble saying 'no' in the moment, follow the 24-hour rule. Tell them, "Let me think about that. Can I get back to you tomorrow?" This will help you process the request and listen to your intuition. Do you really *want* to do what was asked of you, or do you feel *obligated*? Make a choice that pleases you. Ask yourself, 'will I feel drained or energized if I do this?' Only do what makes you feel energized.

4. Set clear standards. If you want others to treat you well, you must first figure out what that looks like for you. Maybe you're tired of people expecting you to volunteer for everything. Maybe you tolerated emotional abuse. Instead of letting others know it hurt your feelings, you might have kept it inside. Maybe you're busy taking care of your kids/parents/friends, going above and beyond at the cost of neglecting your own needs.

Learn to say no (see #2), and set clear boundaries. An easy boundary to begin with is, "Ouch, that hurt." Or, "Don't talk to me that way. I don't like it." By practicing clear boundaries, you will slowly model how you want others to treat you and garner more respect.

Once you've developed an effective self-care ritual, you'll be ready to develop relationships with people who respect you. You'll know how to recognize the qualities of a good person at the start of a relationship, not six months or six years down the road. You will be loved and appreciated because you've modeled how you want others to treat—because you love and respect yourself first.

Step 12: Be firm about your standards

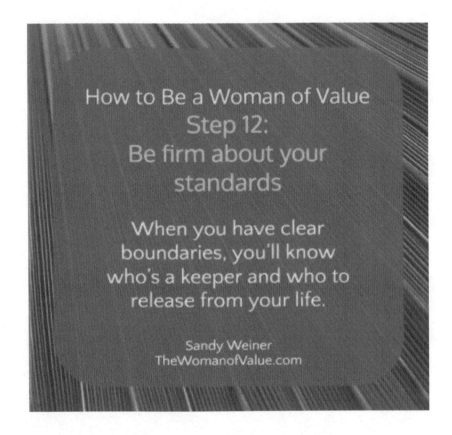

What are boundaries and how will setting them change your life?

Boundaries are our emotional self-defense. They teach people how to treat us. They keep us safe and sane. When you set clear boundaries in love and in life, you preserve your dignity and self-respect. You show your value as a person when you can say 'no' to what doesn't work for you and 'yes' to what does.

This is such a big topic, I co-lead a course on **Boundaries for Beautiful Relationships** with Theresa Byrne. For this chapter, I'm sharing a powerful exercise on setting boundaries in your love life.

How to Set Clear Boundaries in Love

Step 1: Get clear on what you want/need in life and love. Make a list of what you will and won't do in your relationships.

Examples of Setting Personal Boundaries in Dating:

- I will not sleep with someone until _____ happens.

- I will be open to dating _____ types of men.

- I will be open to dating a man who lives _____ distance from me.

- I will be open to dating men who are _____ years older/younger.

Step 2: Clearly and kindly set boundaries.

Examples of Clear Boundaries You Set for Him:

- No texting anything except facts and non-emotional information.

- I'm uncomfortable being kissed before I've developed more trust.

- I want to meet someone from online dating as soon as possible.

- I want to meet for coffee or a drink for a first date (not a 3-hour hike, not a fancy 5-course meal).

- I will kindly end the date when it's going on too long.

- I'm an on time person. How about you?

Step 3: Observe what happens next. How does he respond to your boundary setting?

Quick boundary scripts, things you can say in tough situations.

- I'm not comfortable with _____.

- That doesn't work for me. Can I tell you what works better?

- Ouch.

Here are a few more boundary tips to help you stay safe in dating:

1. If you want to know how a man feels about you, lean back.

We tend to do way too much for men at the beginning of a relationship. If you want to see if a man is invested in getting to know you, lean back. That means don't go to his house before you build trust with him. Don't buy him gifts to win him over when you're just starting to get to know him. Don't anxiously call or text him if he's not putting forth much effort. Lean back to see how HE shows up. If he's investing time and effort in the relationship, you have your answer.

2. If a guy pressures you for sex and doesn't respect your needs, leave him for someone who does.

Personal boundaries around your body and sexuality is extremely important. I'm not saying you should abstain from sex altogether if it's something you want. I want you to have sex with standards; to progress sexually according to your timeline, not out of pressure to meet a guy's needs when it means giving up your own.

3. Stand up for what's important to you.

If something is bothering you, let him know how you feel. Say it in a way he can hear, not in an attacking, labeling, stick-it-to-him fashion. If he's defensive, that's not a good sign. You want to be with someone who respects you and what's important to you, not someone who puts you down as 'too sensitive' or 'too needy' when you take a stand for your needs.

The keys to having standards and dating with dignity start young. These basic tenets don't change much over time. Develop your dating standards. They will serve you well throughout your life.

Exercise: Script Your Dating Standards Around Sex and Exclusivity

Prepare a short script that states your standards, so you're prepared to discuss them with the right man at the right time.

Step 13: Do NOT settle

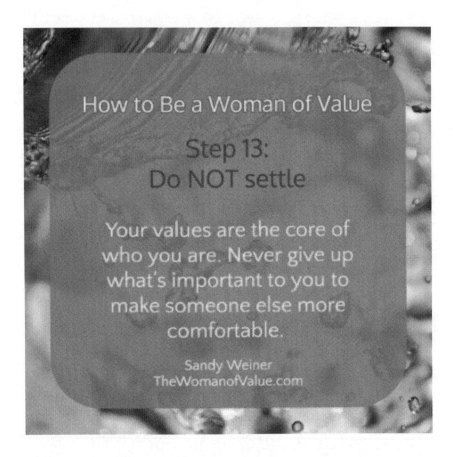

Is it ever okay to settle in a relationship? Let's define the true meaning of settling…

When I first heard about Lori Gottlieb's New York Times bestselling book, **Marry Him: The Case for Settling for Mr. Good Enough**, I was offended. At first glance, the book seemed to be asking women and men to settle in a relationship, to give up what they truly want and need in a mate. Doesn't that set you up for failure? Should you really give up on your dream of meeting and marrying your true love? That's not at all what Lori is talking about.

Ms. Gottlieb, single and forty, had grown frustrated with her search for "Mr. Right". She decided to stop chasing the elusive Prince Charming and get real about finding a husband. She began by observing her happily married friends who had married not-so-perfect men. What made them happy?

Did They Settle?

Many admitted that the men they married were not immediate heart-throbs. Their love and affection grew for their husbands. It was based on shared core values. Qualities such as kindness, consideration, compassion, intelligence; these are the things that great matches are made of. These women gave their future spouses a chance. Their relationships developed in a very solid way, and ultimately they did not feel as if they were settling at all.

Prince Charming? Not in the conventional sense, but these men did become their happily ever after. This perspective for settling for Mr. Good Enough makes very good sense.

Here's what Gottlieb had to say in an interview:

"Many women in their twenties or early thirties are either breaking up with really good guys, or refusing to even go on a first date with a really good guy, because there's not instant "chemistry" or because the guy is kind (but not a mind-reader), successful (but not wealthy enough), cute (but balding), and funny (but not Jon Stewart), and they think there's someone better out there.

So they pass up the 8 in order to hold out for the 10 – and then suddenly they're 38 or 40 and now they can only get a 5. The 8 would have been the catch. Most of us would be very happy married to the 8. But we don't realize this at the time. This whole business of "having it all" is a problem because guess what, most of us aren't 10s either. Some guy is going to have to put up with our flaws and give up certain things he may want in a partner, too.

Maybe he wanted someone taller, or someone with a better sense of humor or someone less sensitive. We tend to forget about that because our female friends are always telling us how fabulous we are, and soon we think we're so fabulous that we always find a reason that this guy or that guy isn't good enough for us.

By acknowledging these truths, you can adjust your behavior so you're not always sitting there wondering why you can't find Mr. Right. If you're like many single women today, you've probably been passing up a lot of Mr. Rights along the way because of these unrealistic expectations."

Why I think this book is important:

1. Many people settle in a relationship. They may think that their partner is as good as it gets. If they are marrying a 7 or 8, perhaps their love will grow with time. But when they compromise on too many of the most important elements of a truly loving union, those marriages usually fail. This is not the "good enough" that Gottlieb is referring to. Focus on the most essential non-negotiable qualities you need in a truly loving compatible connection, and your love will grow over time.

2. Think twice about passing up a perfectly good guy. Judging him based on his job? Education? Height? These things don't necessarily indicate his true nature/ability/intelligence. Focus less on the externals and more on the internal qualities in a potential match.

3. Attraction is based on many unpredictable factors. Gottlieb concludes that we don't always know what we need in a relationship or understand why we are attracted to the opposite sex. We may think we need certain things in a partner, but something totally different will make us happier. We wouldn't know it unless

it hit us in the face. In other words, give the good guys a chance. You may be passing up Mr. Good Enough in your search for what you believe is Mr. Right.

Exercise for Finding Mr. Good Enough

Make a list of your five must-haves and deal breakers. Focus on the qualities in a man that you absolutely can't live without, and for your deal breakers, the qualities you can't live with. (Everything else is a 'nice-to-have', not a 'must-have'.) If a man meets those basic requirements, give the relationship a chance to develop, especially if the attraction is not off the charts. If the chemistry is a ten from the start, run for the hills! You'll probably throw your standards out the window when your brain is hijacked by your hormones.

Be open. Don't turn down a potential match based on a lack of butterflies. Open up your possibility of finding Mr. Right by giving Mr. Good Enough a chance.

Step 14: Declutter your life

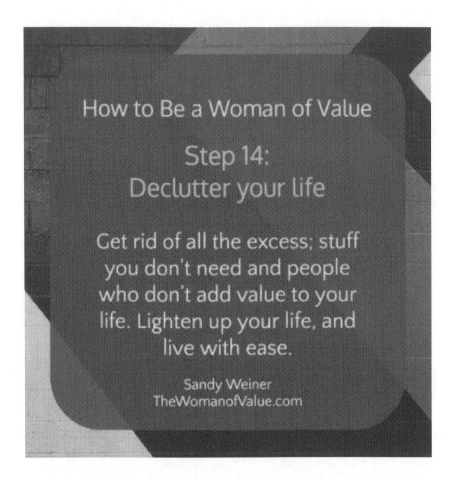

Do you have a hard time throwing things away? Do you fill your home and life with things you don't really need? Clutter can hold you back in your personal and romantic life.

Clutter in your home:

Clutter in the home creates a sense of chaos, heaviness, and can make you feel stuck. I just threw out 12 bags of my family's clothes and shoes, and I feel like I lost 10 pounds! I know someone with a shopping addiction who has so much clothes, she doesn't remember what she has, so she keeps buying the same thing over and over. Can you relate?

Here's how to declutter your home…with an eye on future romance.

The first step in creating a romantic home is a lot like the first step in romance: find out what you love and keep it. Let everything else go. Begin by removing every item from the walls and furniture. Evaluate each item's aesthetic and nostalgic value. Ask, "Does this enrich my life?" Sort the items into three groups: things you love, things you're unsure about, and things you don't care for. Bag the third group and take it immediately to the nearest donation center. Then take the items you love and put them back on the walls and furniture, dusting and rearranging them as needed. Then leave the house for a break and a palette cleanser — get some coffee, go out to lunch or see a movie. When you return, if a few items seem to be calling your name, gather them back up. Otherwise donate or recycle them and don't look back.

Clutter in your friendships:

Maybe you have friendships that are no longer serving you. For example, you have a long time friend who always had a short fuse. As you grew and evolved and worked on yourself, you now notice that she's unkind, and her reactivity makes you very uncomfortable.

Or you have a friend who gossips all the time, and even though you've told her you don't want to talk about other people, she won't stop.

When you've set a boundary with friends and they haven't listened, what they're essentially telling you is that your needs matter less than theirs. With friends like that, who needs enemies…

Clutter in your relationships with men:

You're still in love with your ex, but you don't see him anymore. If you still compare every man you date with him, you've got man-clutter.

Or, you keep all the men you've dated as friends, even if they're not treating you as a friend, you've got man-clutter.

10 Things You Can Do in Your Home to Manifest Your Man

One of my podcast guests, Katie Titi, is the host of Great Men Do Exist, Create a Space for Love, and author of the #1 Amazon Best-selling book, Love By Design: 10 things you can do in your home now to manifest your man.

With a background in love coaching and interior design, Katie specializes in guiding women to redesign their mindsets and environments in compassionate and vigorous support of their romantic love endeavors so they can be the best option for the amazing man that they're meant to attract.

Check out highlights below of episode #264: Love By Design: 10 Things You Can Do to Manifest Your Man.

What are ten things women can do in their homes to manifest love?

People tend to leave their homes in a default mode. When you walk in someone's home, you can tell what their priorities are. I love to light candles. I like rose, lavender, sandalwood and a few others. I leave them out, so I light them more often.

1. *Make sure your self-care items are out and easy to access.*

2. *Put out images/art work of your love life and what you want to manifest.*

3. *Bring nature into your home. A fountain, an image of a beach on desktop or hanging up on a wall.*

4. *Take an audit of your home. Look at the things in your home, and ask yourself if they're serving your goal for finding love. If not, declutter.*

5. *Shift energy in your home by determining what you want to add to your space. Ask yourself, What do I want? And design your home according to that. Live as if you're already where you want to be in love.*

6. *Feng shui tip: have two of everything; a night stand on either side of your bed, two lamps, so there's room for your future man.*

7. *Make space in your closet for a man.*

8. *Add some romantic sculptures.*

9. *Create your own art or vision board, and watch it physically manifest what you desire.*

10. *Make sure your rooms are painted in more inclusive colors, not just pink or feminine colors.*

Exercise to Declutter

Choose one action from the list above that you'll do this week to declutter your home, your friendships, and/or your love life.

Step 15: Be a lifetime learner

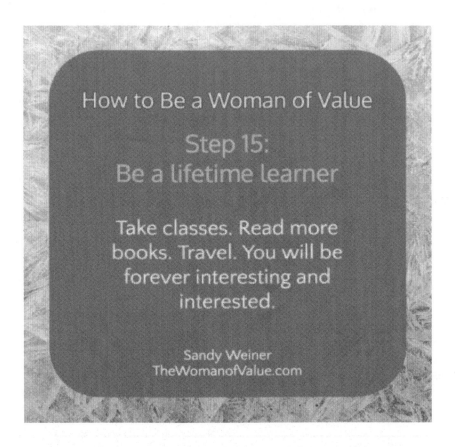

If you want to attract or sustain a relationship with a loving partner, someone who has your must-haves, make sure you have those same must-haves. For many women over 40, one of the items on their must-have list is 'lifetime learner', someone engaged in growing intellectually, curious about learning more throughout their life.

When you actively engage in learning, your mind expands. And as a result, you become more interesting.

Are you a lifetime learner? What are you doing to keep your brain engaged? Are you taking classes? Reading books and articles outside of your comfort zone? If not, I've listed many options for you to get started or add to what you're already doing.

How to Be a lifetime learner

1. Continuing Education: Check out your local continuing ed catalogue for classes in something you've always wanted to learn. Photography? Oil painting? Mastering Microsoft Word or Powerpoint? Sign up for a class and expand your brain!

2. Join a Meetup group: Go to meetup.com and check off your areas of interest. Meetups are great for meeting new people and trying new things. Whether it's a sport you've wanted to try for the first time or get back into after many years on hiatus, or a class you're interested in, meetups have it all. Go to a foreign film with a group and have dinner or drinks after the show. Go to a new exhibit at your local museum with a group.

3. Online education: There are so many ways to expand your education online. I've taken classes to grow my business, create webinars, market, use Instagram and Pinterest. Online classes offer a huge array of classes, and the best part is, you don't have to leave your home. Plus, many offer an online group forum, so you'll connect with likeminded individuals and perhaps make new friends or business connections. I offer several classes in how to understand men, how to overcome fears in dating, and how to find love after 40. Sign up for an online class today!

4. Start your own class: If you can't find what you're looking for, start a class of your own. You probably have more expertise than you know. Are you a great cook or baker? Offer a class for single men on simple meals to prepare at home. You might even meet an eligible bachelor or two!

As you can see, there are many ways to learn and expand your knowledge base. Remember that the more you know, the more interesting you become. And who doesn't want to hang around with an interesting person?

Exercise on Becoming a Lifelong Learner

Pick a class, join a group, read a book, or choose another way to expand your mind. Fill your calendar with social events that expand your brain and make you a very interesting woman!

Step 16: Don't make assumptions

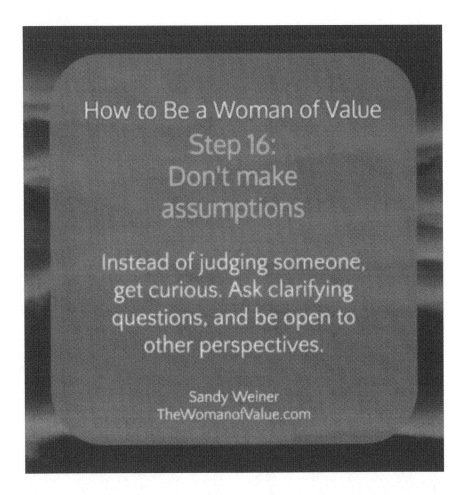

You've probably heard the old adage, "assumptions make an ass of you and me". And while you may *think* you understand how bad it is to make assumptions about people, you're probably still doing it occasionally on a subconscious level. It's hard not to. Our primal brain judges others because it wants to keep us safe. If we sense danger, we keep our distance. And that can be a very good thing.

But it can also be dismal, especially in dating and relationships. Your assumptions might very well be the reason you're still single.

You see the world through your lens, and you interpret your date's actions and words in a way that makes sense to you.

Unless you get curious about what it all means to HIM or HER, you are likely to misinterpret and misunderstand your date's very essence. And guess what? You're probably missing out on some amazing potential matches due to your assumptions. And if they make assumptions about you, they're missing out on getting to know a pretty awesome person, right? I'll bet you dislike being misunderstood and prematurely judged as much as I do.

Yes, I'm a dating coach for women over 40. I'm also dating after my divorce, and I'm very self-aware when it comes to things like assumptions in dating. But…

I, too, have been caught in the "assumption trap". I'm eating humble pie as I share what happened to me a few years ago.

I went on a very challenging hike with a group from meetup.com. I didn't know a single person in the group, but I wanted to meet new people and get my heart pumping outdoors. The weather was absolutely gorgeous.

The hike was led by "George", a good looking guy in his late forties, tanned, a real jock. He organizes many outdoor events throughout the year, and judging by his appearance and manner, I had made an assumption that he must not be very deep. Smart maybe, but not brilliant. A little aloof. Life of the party type, an extrovert. I assumed he was single, but I wasn't sure that a guy like him was "marriage material".

I had a wonderful time on the hike, and when I returned home, I received a thank-you email from the group. It included the profiles of all the attendees, so I checked out a few profiles of the lovely people I'd met that day. When I checked out George's Facebook profile, I was shocked.

He was *nothing* like I had assumed.

He seemed to be thoughtful and kind. His writing indicated depth and emotional intelligence. In fact, he shared a heart-wrenching post about his son.

"20 years ago today, I welcomed into this world my first child. Any parent will understand the love that a father has for his children. This was long before I knew what parental alienation was and the price I would pay for divorcing the woman I once loved. What comes to mind is the lyrics from Against the Wind - "I wish I didn't know now what I didn't know then." Happy 20th birthday "A". I love you and always will."

Wow, right? These are not the words of a shallow jock. They are the words of a sensitive loving father. At least that's how I see it. Of course, I might be making an assumption :)

I admit it, even a self-aware woman like me can sometimes make assumptions. I learned my lesson and will think about George the next time I go on a first date.

Exercise to Overcome Assumptions

Be open when meeting people for the first time. Approach every person as a clean slate, and don't bring along the pain of your past relationships. Be curious. If you don't understand something they said, or you get triggered, ask questions. Don't assume anything. You wouldn't want to make an ass of you and me, right?

Step 17: Let go of toxic people

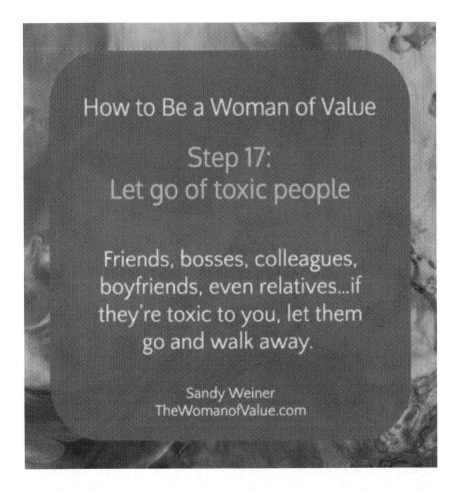

How to Be a Woman of Value

Step 17:
Let go of toxic people

Friends, bosses, colleagues, boyfriends, even relatives...if they're toxic to you, let them go and walk away.

Sandy Weiner
TheWomanofValue.com

Sugar and spice and everything nice, that's what little girls are made of...

From the time we're little, most women are taught to be kind to everyone. Kindness is lovely, but being nice to all people at all times? That's not a good idea. If you're being kind without boundaries, some people are going to treat you poorly and take advantage of your kind nature. There's a high cost to being nice no matter what.

In the dating world, nice can be toxic. It may sound like a contradiction, but...

- How many times have you been nice when you were not really interested in a guy?

- Stayed on the phone with a man longer than you wanted to, just to be nice?

- Didn't say no to a good night kiss (or more) when you were not attracted or not ready, because you wanted to be seen as the nice girl?

- Or worse, put up with a guy who was mistreating you because you thought setting limits was unkind and might push him away?

What is the right kind of 'nice' in the dating world?

Nice is about being polite, saying please and thank you, and asking a man about his life instead of focusing only on your own.

It's also about breaking up with someone without hurting their feelings. If you're dating online, nice can be writing a kind reply to a man who doesn't interest you but took the time to write a substantial message.

Nice can mean being careful not to burn your bridges when you break up with someone. Maybe down the road, a man you're dating who isn't right for you now will be right for you or a friend in the future. If you are unkind now, you may ruin your prospects for a second chance later on. Always take the high road in life and love!

When is being nice not in your best interest?

When a man always calls you at the last minute for a date, and you say yes, that's not being nice. When you drop plans with friends to be with this guy, you may think you're being 'nice' to him, but you're unkind to your friends and especially to yourself.

Here's what you risk: This man sees you as having low standards, and you are setting yourself up to be treated poorly by him in the future. Your friends see you as an inconsiderate friend, making last-minute-Joe your first priority instead of them. These are your long-term pals who really love you. And over time, after he rejects you because he doesn't really value you, you will probably see that you've lost out on your own self-dignity (and may have lost a few close friends in the process).

Stop being so nice to...

Stop being nice to anyone who doesn't have your best interest in mind, who doesn't honor and respect you, even when they disagree. Walk away from anyone who puts your needs last, who puts you at the bottom of their list.

It's not always easy to set standards for yourself as to how you want to be treated by others. But it is an essential first step in living and loving as a woman of value.

As my friend Jen says, "My level of commitment cannot exceed yours". Make sure there's a balance of give and take. When you're giving way more than you're receiving, you're going to be depleted and resentful.

Exercise: Journal About a Toxic Relationship

Take as long as you need to journal about a time when you thought you were being nice to someone, and that person ended up being toxic to you. What was the situation? Where were you? Why did you keep being kind when that person didn't appreciate you?

Can you see an opportunity where you could have set boundaries? If so, what boundary would you set if you were to get a do-over?

There's a right way to be nice. It should never be at the risk of losing yourself in a relationship that's toxic to you.

Step 18: Dare to think big

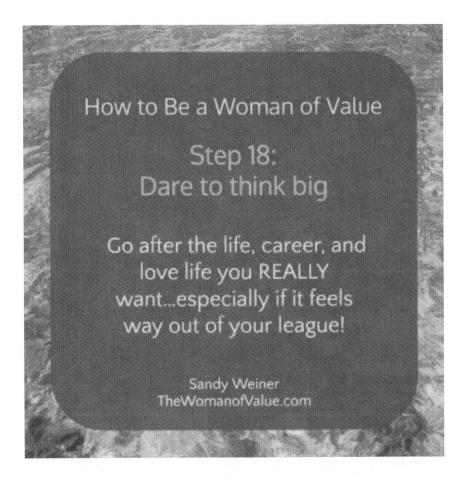

"If you don't go after what you want, you'll never have it.

If you don't ask, the answer is always no.

If you don't step forward, you're always in the same place."

- Nora Roberts

I love this quote. Because I spent most of my first five decades of life not dreaming bigger, not taking those big risks and getting way out of my comfort zone to live the life I was meant to live.

Think bigger and ask for what you want? That can be scary. What if someone says no—to your request for a promotion, to having your book published, or even to being the first to say 'I love you'? Rejection can be painful. So we stay safe in our little cozy cocoon. But…what's the downside of never thinking bigger and asking for what you want?

You stay in a job where you're unhappy and dread going to work. You stay in a relationship that is stale, or worse— emotionally, verbally, or even physically abusive.

When it comes to growing bigger in life and love, you've got to leave your comfort zone and ask for what you REALLY want.

Yes, growth can be painful. But if you don't ask for what you want, you'll stagnate. You will not get what you deserve. And like Nora Roberts says, you'll always end up in the same place, and the answer will always be no.

How many times have you been too afraid to ask for what you wanted? And what happened when you didn't speak up? I've been there, done that, too. Before I learned how to speak up for myself, I was too shy to ask for what I wanted. And I lost so many opportunities.

Case study

When I was in my late twenties, I met an amazing man. I fell in love almost immediately. He had everything I thought I needed and wanted in a husband – a good job, a generous heart, and a great personality. He was funny and we liked the same books and movies. We both played guitar and sang. We played racquetball together on the weekends, and went to concerts in Greenwich

Village during the week. Most important, he had a steel core of integrity. He was honest, philanthropic, and good-hearted. I thought about him during the day and dreamt about him every night.

There was only one problem. After two months, there was still no first kiss. No holding hands. The relationship was platonic, and I was going a little crazy. I thought he must be a little shy, a slow mover, someone for whom friendship was the basis of a solid relationship. I was patient. I could wait if it meant long-term love, maybe even marriage!

And then, he called to invite me over for a home-cooked meal. I was so excited. This is going to be the night, I thought. The anticipation was titillating. I can still taste the delicious spinach quiche and salad he lovingly prepared for me. When he brought out the home-baked apple pie, I was swooning. Unfortunately, I had a bad headache, so he offered massage on his bed. With the door shut. Oh my god! His touch was exquisite. This is it, I thought, finally, our first kiss.

The massage ended. I got up from the bed. He just stood there with his hands in his pockets. No kiss. Nothing. Nada. Not even a hug. I thought, "maybe he just needs a sign from me? Maybe I'm giving him the idea that I just want to be friends?" so I walked over, a big warm smile on my face, and gave him a hug. What happened next was pivotal to the next 25 years of my life.

He did not kiss me. In fact, I felt his body recoil. I was humiliated. I had opened myself up and become vulnerable. I had taken a risk with that hug and he shut me down. He wouldn't even walk me home. I was mortified. I left that night feeling dejected and ashamed. We never spoke about it. And we stopped being friends. About a month later, I found out he was engaged. Engaged! It turns out, he had been dating her all along, and I had a whole different story in my head. I thought we were heading towards an amazing relationship. What a shock.

I shut my heart down on that day. I vowed to never again risk being so attached to a man I liked.

I now know that was the wrong conclusion. As a woman dating today, I would have talked to him about it. I would have asked for what I wanted and needed. I would have known early on whether he was dating me or just hanging out as friends. And I certainly would not have fallen in love with a man who didn't want what I wanted.

What does this story have to do with asking for what you want?

A few years later, this man came back into my life. My husband met him in synagogue, and he invited him and his wife to our home for dinner. This turned into a decades long friendship.

One day, his wife told me she had met him through a setup at a mutual friend's wedding. After the reception ended, he accompanied her back to her hotel in a taxi, and he said, "If you're ever in New York again, look me up." She thought, "No way I'm letting this guy go." She went back to her friend and told her, "I want to marry this guy. Make sure he asks me out again." **Here was a woman who asked for what she wanted and got it!**

Exercise on Asking for What You Want

- What's something you really want, but you're afraid to go for it? Write it down.

- Why do you want it? When you know your 'why', it's easier to overcome your fear of taking a risk and putting yourself out there.

- What's one small step you can take to get what you want? Write that down.

- Do you need to contact someone to get what you want? Find that person, and ask for what you want.

What's the worst that could happen? You might get a 'no'. And that's okay. But, you also might get a 'YES'. If you don't risk, you don't get to live that big juicy beautiful life you deserve. Go for it!

Step 19: Choose love over fear

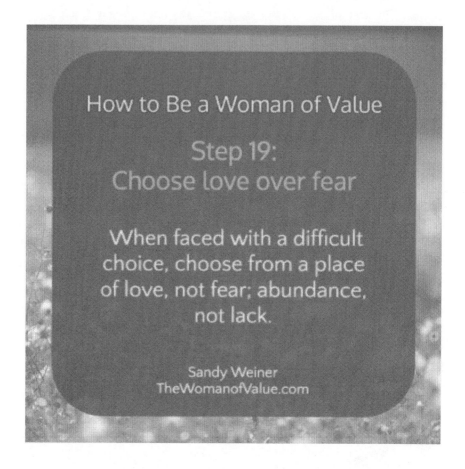

You've had difficult choices to make in life. Who to marry, when to have children (or not have kids), when to move, where to move to, which job to take, which school to go to, which friends to let go of, how to parent, how to take care of your parents....AH!!!

So many choices in life, and you've gotten this far, haven't you? The earth didn't open and swallow you up for making the 'wrong' choice, did it?

Yet, many people are paralyzed about making difficult choices. They don't trust that things will work out, so they push off a decision and avoid taking a risk. They don't move to that new location, even though there will be incredible opportunities there for a new job, for personal growth, for meeting new people, for finding love.

Why do we avoid making those difficult decisions? Fear. We're afraid of failing, of being alone, of not making new friends, of being passed over for that job promotion.

So, we take the safe choice. We stay in a job that is sucking the life out of us. We stay in awful relationships, even though we feel more alone with this person. We don't speak up, we don't move on. But, what if we did play a bigger game? What if we did speak up, move to that new city, change jobs, go to that party, talk to a stranger? We might get passed over for that promotion, not like our new job, or be ignored by that stranger.

And we might NOT! What would it feel like to rise up in your career? What would it feel like to wake up every day and LOVE your job, love your partner, love your LIFE?

What would you be giving up if you were to NOT have those things in your life? You'd risk being truly happy and fulfilled. And that would be a shame. So, choose from a place of love, not fear.

Here's how:

When faced with a difficult choice, feel the fear. What are you afraid of? Go deeper into what would happen if you made that choice. The worst possible thing? Go there!

Now, go deeper. And then what? And then what? And then what?

What usually happens, is we eventually see that the fear was all in your head.

F.E.A.R. is an acronym for False Evidence Appearing Real.

Yes, fear can be real and can help keep us safe from harm, especially when there's a safety threat, like when you're in true danger of getting hurt.

However, the type of fear I'm talking about here is one where there's no true threat of immediate physical danger, no real threat of loss of someone or something you love. This type of **F.E.A.R.** is an illusion. It's something we fabricate in our minds and imagine is real.

John's story

When I first started coaching, I worked with people in midlife to help them make their passions and dreams come true. One of my first clients was a man we'll call John, who always dreamed of having his own restaurant. He wanted to make it a reality, but was deeply afraid of failure. He had worked in the food industry all his life, and he had the smarts and funding to make this dream a reality. The only thing holding him back was—his fear!

I took him through the exercise above.

"What would happen if you failed?" I asked.

"I'd lose all my money", he said.

"And then what would happen?" I asked.

"I'd be homeless", he said.

"And then what would happen?" I asked.

"I'd live on the street with my family," he said.

And then he burst out laughing.

"What's so funny?" I asked.

"That would never happen", he said. "I would never lose all my money or be homeless. I'm way too responsible to let that happen."

He realized that his fear had been driving the ship for way too long, and it was time to make his dream come true.

A year later, he opened 'The Silver Lining Restaurant', a perfect name for someone whose dream had become a reality. The only thing stopping him had been fear. When he came from a place of love, he was unstoppable.

Exercise: Choosing Love Over Fear

Keep a journal. For the next week, for every decision you make, consciously choose to come from a place of love, not fear.

For example, when eating a healthy breakfast, tell yourself, "I choose this healthy meal, because I love my body and want to treat it with care."

If you were coming from fear, the conversation would go more like this: "I choose this healthy meal, because I don't want to get fat." Or, "I want to lose weight, so those foods are not permitted to me." Or, "I must starve myself and eat foods I don't really like."

Over time, your brain will be biased towards love and not fear. Writing about how you feel with each decision made from love will help you see how far you've come.

Step 20: Adapt a positive mindset

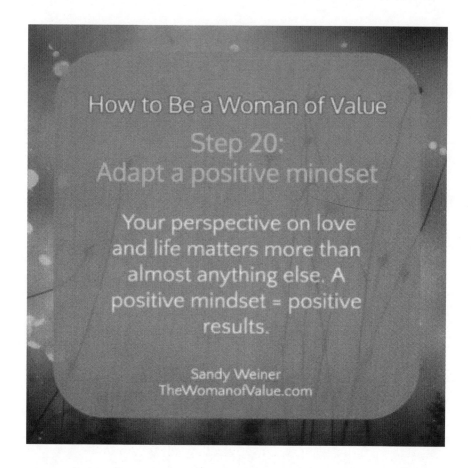

The #1 key to having the life and love you want is a positive mindset.

If you're a single woman, dating can be exhausting, and the prospect of rejection can make you choose the safest path, which is never leaving the house and going out on dates. That way, you can't get hurt, right?

Well, perhaps nothing bad will happen, but what about the good stuff? It's going to be pretty hard to experience a loving partnership unless you're prepared to go on dates. Adopting a positive mindset with dating will not only boost your confidence about finding the right person, but by being positive in your dating approach, you will bring good energy to dates. That energy will shine through and make you even more irresistible to the right partner.

Two things you can do to adapt a positive mindset

1. Say 'YES' to the 'MAYBE's'

One specific way to approach dating positively is to adopt a more positive attitude about WHO you date. Think of all those dates you've refused to go on, those blind dates that you wouldn't take part in, the party invites you declined. Where has this led you in your search for love? Nowhere. But if you said 'yes' to the 'maybe's instead, what's the worst that could happen?

Many people shy away from saying 'yes' to a person who invites them on a date, because they don't happen to tick all the boxes on their ideal partner list, or because they fear it will not go well. Bear in mind that you're only looking for one special person, and your idea of that perfect partner could be all wrong. Saying 'yes' to a date who is a 'maybe' is a great idea. You never know if that 'maybe' will turn into a 'yes' for you.

All you need to do is get over the hurdle of that first meeting, and you'll soon know if you're on the right track. Of course, you should always take sensible precautions when meeting someone new – opting for a busy and public venue.

You'll soon know how you feel about a person, but how do you judge what they think of you? Sometimes, it's obvious in the way they interact with you or whether they suggest another date.

However, if you're having difficulty gauging what your date thinks of you, check out signs from their body language. You can tell a lot about a person from their posture, eye contact and the way they handle themselves in your company.

2. Don't give up after a string of bad first dates.

It would be unusual to find your perfect partner on your first date. You may be lucky, but don't count on it. People on the dating scene often get disillusioned if they have a string of dates that don't work out or don't lead to any type of relationship.

The old saying about 'plenty of fish in the sea' is a good perspective for your dating mindset. Life rarely turns out the way it does in fairy tales or Hollywood movies, with boy meeting girl as if by magic. Sparks don't usually fly. In fact, if they do, it's a pretty good sign that the relationship will crash and burn. Look for chemistry AND compatibility. It can take time and many dates before finding someone with whom you really click.

If your date is not interested in you, or vice versa, chalk it up to a learning experience and move on. Don't waste any time brooding over what could have been. Instead look forward to the next date. Remember, all it takes is one special person.

Keep up your dating momentum and positive mindset and you'll meet the right person soon enough. And when you do, you'll be able to think back and remember all those other dates that finally got you to your last first date!

Exercise to Create a More Positive Mindset

Whenever you have a negative thought, stop for a moment. Bring your awareness to that thought. Ask yourself, "Is this 100% true?" If it's not true, find contrary evidence. Ask yourself, "When did I experience that this wasn't true?" Next substitute a positive thought instead. Do that throughout your day, and you'll soon become a much more positive thinker, leading to positive outcomes in your love life.

*This exercise is based on the brilliant work of Byron Katie. For more information, go to https://thework.com/

PILLAR III: SPEAK UP

"Speaking up for the truth isn't always easy. It takes courage, but it's necessary."

Amber Valletta

Step 21: Your past doesn't limit you

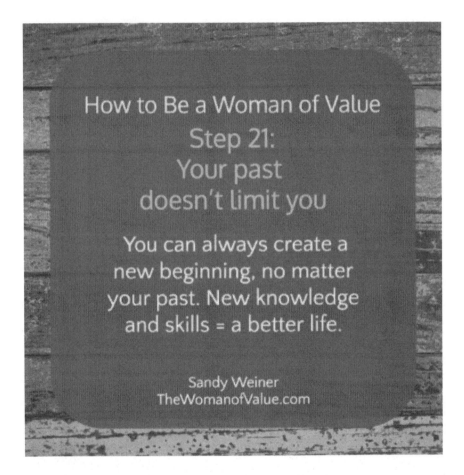

Many people feel limited by their past. They believe they're doomed because of their upbringing, their past relationships, or their past pain. While it's true that your past helped to form who you are today, it's also true that you get to choose how you process past pain. You get to choose who you want to be and how you want to show up from this day forward.

I had a client who was a people pleaser. When we first started working, she told me, "I can't help being a people pleaser. It's in my DNA". She learned to be a people pleaser at home. It was her way to receive love growing up in a dysfunctional home. She continued to over-give throughout her life. But is it hard-wired into her DNA? I don't think so. I believe it's a habit. We can break habits that don't serve us any longer. And I helped her do just that.

She was in debt because of her chronic people-pleasing. She had to learn to stop giving away her money to people she felt sorry for. Through the work we did together, she found love and married for the first time in her late 50s. And it was all about not letting her past determine her present and future.

That's what's wonderful about identifying what's holding you back. Once you figure that out, you can actually do something about it. You have so much power to change your future!

I grew up with a mother who was a self-confessed martyr. She'd do nice things for people, and it would take its toll on her. She was often exhausted and resentful. She often felt people were taking advantage of her. This is so common. People pleasing, over-giving, over-doing, and burnout, resentment, exhaustion. Can you relate?

As an adult, when I became healthier emotionally and mentally, I had a conversation with her about her martyrdom. She said, "I come from a long line of martyrs. I can't help it. It's just who I am."

She had learned this unhealthy behavior pattern from her mother, who probably learned it from her mother. When you give from a place of obligation and not choice, you can easily build up resentment. I was stuck in that pattern for a long time, too. But, once I became more self-aware, I vowed to live my life differently.

I told my mother, "I also come from a long line of martyrs. And I've chosen not to be one anymore."

That was a defining moment for me. I knew I could live my life in integrity, aligned with who I am, not with what others expected of me. I knew that if I lived my life in this way, I'd be happier, and eventually, I'd attract in my best partner. (Someone who was also immersed in self-care and self-awareness, a reformed people-pleaser perhaps?).

Where have you been hurt in the past?

If you've ever been fired from a job, it stings. But, did you say to yourself, "I'm just not meant to work"? No, I'll bet you dusted yourself off and got hired again. I'll also bet your next job was a better fit, and getting fired was a blessing in disguise.

Same goes for failed relationships. It doesn't matter if you have been dumped, divorced, or widowed. You can find a lasting loving relationship, especially if you are self-reflective and have learned how to do better next time.

With the right inner work, you can accomplish so much more than you ever imagined. So don't let your past limit you. Take one action step today to move forward with a more vibrant future.

Exercise: Letting Go of Your Past

- In your journal, ask yourself: "What's a story or belief I'm holding onto from my past?"

- Some examples might be: I can never get a promotion. I always attract unavailable men. Men always leave me. Everyone is selfish. People take advantage of my good nature.

- Once you've identified a story or belief, ask yourself, "What am I gaining by holding onto this story?" Some benefits might be: My heart won't get broken. I won't get rejected. I get to be right.

- Now, ask yourself, "What will I gain by letting go of this limiting belief/story?"

- Some gains might be: I will find the love I always wanted. I will have deeper relationships. I will be happier.

Repeat this practice with any story or limiting belief you're holding onto until you've let go of all the stories that have been holding you back. It will feel amazing to be free of the past!

Step 22: Communicate clearly and graciously

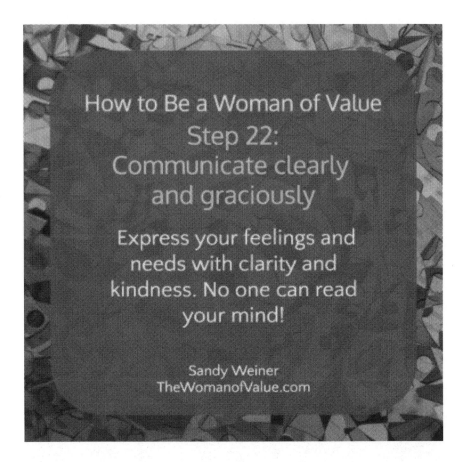

A woman of value knows how to speak her mind. She doesn't expect anyone to read her mind and guess what she's thinking. Her communication is clear. She asks for what she wants, and she does it with grace.

If you don't express your feelings and needs, you will not get what you want. When you know how to express your feelings and needs with clarity, you will have better relationships with everyone.

Throughout my marriage, my ex-husband would shy away from conflict or confrontation. On many occasions, when something needed to be discussed, I would try to talk to him, and he'd shut me out. I now know there's a term for that—stonewalling. We'd be taking a walk in our neighborhood, and I'd bring up something important. He would stop, tell me me he didn't want to talk about it, and then turn away from me and walk home alone.

I felt like I had been slapped in the face or had a door shut on me. Over time, I stopped bringing up difficult issues. I would talk things out with friends instead. My ex and I grew more and more distant until the loneliness and disconnect became unbearable for me. A marriage without clear and effective communication cannot survive.

One of the gifts of my divorce is my ex-husband finally agreed he needed help with his communication skills. He found the support he needed through non-violent communication, a system taught by Dr. Marshall Rosenberg. He finally had a way to process his feelings and needs!

The last three years of our marriage, we were separated and living in the same house on separate floors. The new communication skills made those three years so much better. We were finally at peace, able to talk out our issues. As a result, our divorce was much more amicable than I ever dreamed it would be. I could never live with him, but I now know how to speak his language, and he's much more receptive to having a difficult conversation.

When I begin teaching communication skills to my clients, I ask them how something they experienced made them feel. They will often say something like, "I felt like he was mean to me." That's not a feeling. It's an observation or assessment about what he was doing.

So, I say, "How did you feel when he did that to you?" And eventually, with some coaching, she can name the feeling of anger or sadness or frustration, or whatever it is that she feels.

It's liberating to be able to name your feelings. Once you know what they are, you can begin to identify your needs. A woman of value can easily speak about how she feels and what needs were unmet. She can then make a request of the person who hurt her.

When you feel hurt, it's important to gracefully and powerfully stand up for yourself. When I was younger, I struggled with how to express myself when I felt hurt, especially by a man. I hoped men would be able to read my mind (hah!). I'd tolerate hurtful behaviors until I couldn't take it anymore. Then, I'd explode in anger, giving him a piece of my mind! Wrong, wrong, wrong.

Luckily, I've learned new skills around communication that keep a man connected, not running in the other direction. Empowered communication is one of the cornerstones to a healthy relationship. So, whether you're single and dating or in a long-term relationship/marriage, these tips can help strengthen your relationships.

Exercise: 5 Steps to Speaking Up When Feelings Are Hurt

1. Check in to see if it's a good time to talk. If you speak to him without checking in first, you might as well be speaking to a wall. He won't hear you. When you ask whether it's a good time for him to talk, you're showing you respect him and want his full attention. Men tend to be single-task oriented. If you start talking when he's immersed in another task, he won't hear you.

2. Strip down your issue to an objective statement. Figure out the main issue. What is hurtful? What are you upset about? Strip it down to the core. No judgment. Just the facts. Talk about one thing at a time, not a whole litany of complaints. That's a surefire way to shut anyone down.

3. Use an "I" statement. Don't accuse. Say how you feel.

For example: "When you did _____, I felt _____. It was hurtful to me because _____."

4. Check in again. "How do you feel about what I said?"

5. Come up with a mutually agreed upon resolution. Discuss what you would like him to do differently next time (because there is usually a next time). Brainstorm together to come up with a plan. "I'm sorry" is not enough. "Here's what I'll do next time" is a much better way to resolve the issue.

Next time you feel hurt by anyone, try this 5-step method. And make sure to practice communicating your feelings and needs with everyone in your life. Practice, practice, practice. It will become much more natural to you as you continue to speak up.

Step 23: Be aware of your tone

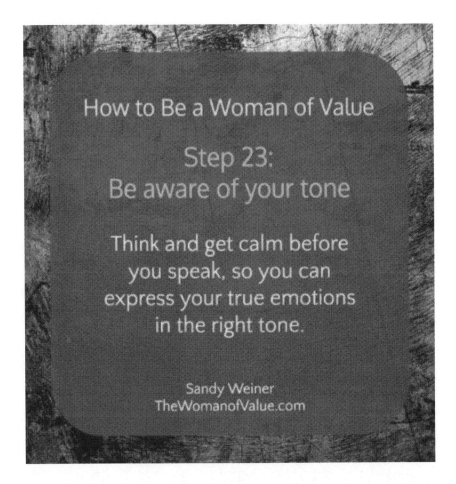

How to Be a Woman of Value

Step 23:
Be aware of your tone

Think and get calm before
you speak, so you can
express your true emotions
in the right tone.

Sandy Weiner
TheWomanofValue.com

Most of us are not great at expressing ourselves when feelings are hurt. Our adrenal system kicks in, and we react with our fight, flight, or freeze response. When we speak from a place of anger and reactivity, we alienate others.

When I was parenting my young children, I worked really hard at not yelling. When my kids misbehaved, I managed to keep from screaming most of the time. What I didn't realize was that my tone of voice was just as upsetting to my kids. I might as well have been yelling.

Luckily, my kids are honest. They told me how they felt about my tone. And it was a gift. I learned how to process my anger and work on my tone. Here's an exercise to help you manage your tone of voice so you can have more loving conversations.

Exercise: Setting the Right Tone

1. Think of a recent experience when your feelings were hurt.

2. Feel whatever emotion(s) you felt at the time, such as anger or frustration

3. Go deeper into that emotion, and feel it in your body. Where do you feel it? Is it in your chest? Your abdomen? A tightness around your heart. Feel it as fully as you can.

4. Place a hand on that part of your body. What's the sensation? Is it tight? Is your heart beating rapidly? Does your stomach hurt?

5. Deepen that feeling. Amp it up by 50%.

6. Deepen it even more, by another 20%. Really feel it.

7. Now, say out loud, "Is this a good time to talk?"

8. Notice your tone of voice. That's probably what you sound like when you're upset or triggered, and you're trying to communicate your needs.

9. Now, take a breath and shake out your body and stretch.

10. Repeat the exercise (steps 1-9), with a more positive emotion, such as gratitude or joy.

11. Notice your tone, your body sensations, and anything else that shifts for you when you embody the positive emotion.

When you communicate tough feelings, it's important to come back to center. If we don't process first and get to a calmer state, we bring negativity to the conversation. This pushes people away. It makes them defensive instead of bringing them closer.

Practice calming yourself with this exercise before having a difficult conversation. If you need to take a time out before speaking up, let the other person know. It's respectful to take care of yourself and manage your anger or hard feelings before discussing a heated issue.

When you come to neutral first, you remove the anger from your voice. You speak from a more constructive and compassionate place, which creates more connection and love.

Step 24: Practice saying NO

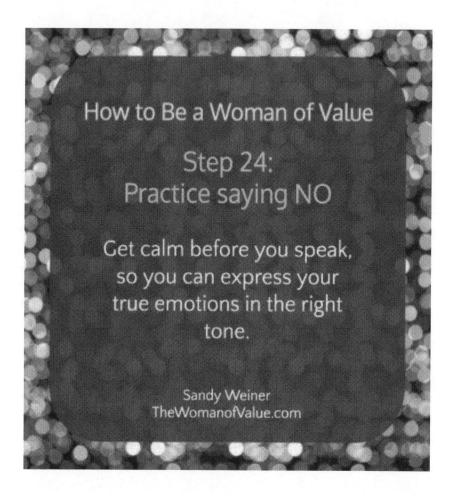

When you respect yourself by saying 'no' and set healthy boundaries, you will give and receive love with an open heart. How hard is it for you to say 'no'? I was raised to do for others, no matter what. Saying 'no' wasn't really an option. You baked, you had guests over, and you helped the sick, even if you were exhausted.

If you say 'yes' when you mean 'no' over and over, it will take its toll on you. You will not be honoring your own needs, and if you do that long enough, you will eventually lose bits of yourself.

If you have trouble saying 'no', it's important to set clear boundaries. I was honored to interview an expert in boundary-setting, Theresa Byrne. She's a martial arts expert who shared important tips on how to set healthy boundaries in relationships on my radio show, Last First Date Radio.

Theresa is a natural protector-power expert who loves seeing people find their innate power. She's a 4th Degree Master Black Belt, the owner of a Colorado martial arts & fitness center, and creator of a self-defense keychain tool. She's the author of "InPower: 3 Ways to Unleash Your Superpowers", has a B.A. in Communication (with concentrations in Psychology/Social Work/ Crisis Intervention and Business/Marketing) and is also a C.M.T focused in sports, kinesiology and healing.

Theresa's also a nationally recognized defense expert teaching on SPIKE TV and several national television programs, and a writer with The Good Men Project and Huffington Post.

Following are loosely transcribed highlights of my interview with Theresa.

The Secrets to Setting Healthy Boundaries in Relationships

What's the biggest mistake people make when it comes to boundaries?

We all grew up learning boundaries, but we didn't learn them well. Unless you learned what healthy boundaries look like, it's hard to set your own healthy boundaries.

What are the top three mistakes people make when it comes to boundaries?

1. You assume boundaries will set themselves. They don't.

2. You set hard boundaries when you're angry. That's a bad time to set boundaries, because you're not thinking straight. You're in flight or fight mode. Set boundaries when you're calm.

3. You assume someone is toxic and label them. Boundaries are a practice to help keep us **safe, sacred, and sane**. This person may be toxic for you, but don't paint them with a label. When you paint someone as toxic, you're blaming.

You're the good guy/hero and the other person is bad. Therefore, there's nothing to learn. There are lessons to be learned in every relationship from every person.

How do you know if a person is toxic for you?

Someone is toxic for you if they drain you, make you feel insecure, small, or that you're not good enough. You feel socked in the gut. Pay attention to your brilliant **intuition**.

The most important thing I'll say is that when someone crosses your boundary, they're saying that what they want is more important than what you want or need. They are telling you they don't care. Walk away from people like that and set a boundary!

What's a boundary you can practice in online dating?

One boundary can be about not giving out your last name. Or maybe it's about meeting someone in a public place. If a guy doesn't respect those boundaries, walk away.

What are some red flags to look out for in a relationship?

If someone moves too fast, it's a red flag. They start telling you how wonderful and amazing you are, that they love you and you're their soul mate. They push you into intimacy before you're ready. It can happen so fast and feel so good, you don't always realize what's happening.

What kind of boundary scripts can you have in your back pocket so you're ready when you're triggered?

These are some great boundary scripts you can have ready:

1. That doesn't work for me.

2. I'm not really comfortable with that.

3. Ouch.

4. This feels awkward.

These lines help you take a step back and gather your thoughts.

And here's my favorite quote from Theresa:

"Your greatest defense weapon is your heart. Your love. We were taught to protect it and guard it. No! Fill yourself up with your self-love and you will not have to guard yourself. You'll live open-heartedly. Your love is your greatest power."

Don't give to get. Share your heart because you want to. Our hearts are connected to an infinite source of love. Your heart will guide you.

Exercise to Just Say No!

Journal about a 'no' you need to set with someone in your life.

*   What's the situation you want to say no around?

*   What feelings come up for you around this situation?

*   What would you like to have happen instead?

- Why is it important to you?

- What's a boundary you want to set to change the situation?

- What are the consequences you're willing to enforce if your boundary is not respected?

- What's the conversation you're willing to have with this person?

Step 25: Know when to say YES

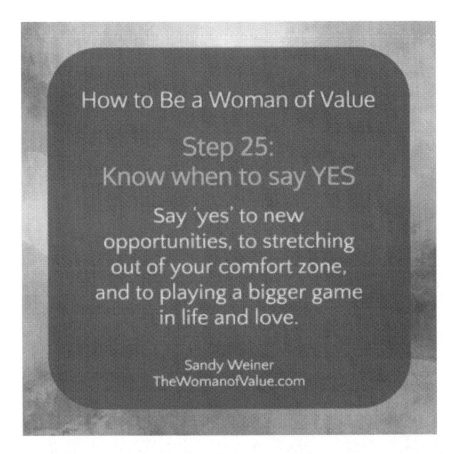

If you want to be more authentic and live your best life, it's important to take risks, leave your comfort zone, and say YES to opportunities that come your way.

This is a story about how I gave my first TEDx talk in 2013. It's about pushing yourself way out of your comfort zone to achieve a goal. It's about not giving up, even though every pore of your body is saying, "I can't do this". It's about stretching yourself beyond what you think is possible, and how that helps you rise up to 'be so good, they can't ignore you', as Steve Martin has said. But this is really not about my TEDx talk. It's about you. It's about hope. And it's about finding love again.

How Did I Land a TEDx Talk?

The short answer is: Five years of hard work.

The longer answer is: I walk almost every day with a good friend. One day, back in early December 2012, I mentioned how much I loved Brenè Brown's TED talk on the power of vulnerability. She said, "What's TED?" I explained that TED was a non-profit organization devoted to ideas worth spreading. The annual TED conference is a prestigious event, and some of the top speakers in the world have delivered amazing speeches that have inspired me.

Two days later, she saw a post on her Facebook wall by a friend who was organizing a TEDx event. These are local TED events, organized all over the world. Her friend posted, 'Do you know anyone who's passionate about something? I'm looking for speakers for my TEDx conference in April.'

My friend, who would not have had a clue what a TEDx was, immediately thought of me. She connected me with the organizer via Facebook messaging.

I submitted a proposal, it was accepted, and then I...FREAKED OUT!!

I was filled with so much fear and tons of limiting beliefs:

1. How could I deliver a talk at such an important conference? I am not a seasoned speaker like everyone else at TEDx.

2. My ideas are not unique. They are not worth spreading. (That was a recurring sabotaging thought).

3. I am terrified of public speaking...without notes...with lights shining in my face...with cameras rolling...with hundreds of people in the audience. Yikes!!

I recovered from the initial panic and took a deep breath. I realized I didn't have to do this talk alone. I could get support. That took a huge weight off my shoulders. I hired a speech coach. She helped me stay focused so I could stick to one theme (I have a tendency to see connections in everything, and had to work hard on taking things out of my speech to keep it clear).

I joined <u>Toastmasters International</u>, an organization devoted to helping people become effective speakers and better leaders.

I worked on my speech for four months, driving my friends and family a little crazy as I rehearsed in front of them. Then I went back and edited again and again. I rehearsed in front of Toastmasters, a divorce support group, my hairdresser, and in front of my wonderful friends again. Oh, and in front of the mirror, in the car, and in an empty stairwell.

I fought my fears. I stretched way beyond my comfort zone. And I triumphed. When the event finally arrived that Friday in April, I was ready (even though I made huge edits the night before...at midnight!).

How Overcoming Fears Can Improve Your Love Life

TEDx was a goal that was so far out of my comfort zone, I didn't think I could do it. I was afraid of looking like a fool. I thought I'd forget my speech, my voice would shake, I'd look stiff. I was worried I'd sound flat and not be engaging.

Growing up, I was the kid in school who was so quiet and reserved, I didn't raise my hand. I was shy. For our ninth grade play, Peter Pan, I was given three words to say, and even that scared me.

A TEDx talk was a HUGE stretch for me.

Taking big risks and moving past your comfort zone stretches you to places you never knew were possible. It grows your confidence by leaps and bounds, and it gets you ready for the next challenge. You learn that you're much more capable than you thought.

How Does this Improve Your Love Life?

When you believe in yourself, you make much better choices in a mate. You attract higher quality people into your life. I was a victim of failed relationships for most of my life. I am a child of divorce. I got divorced myself. But I set out to learn how to have success at love and relationships this time around.

I researched how to be a better date, and most importantly, I learned how to be a better person. I took risks; with online dating, by getting out and socializing with strangers, by moving past my comfort zone and attending singles events. I got out of my house, I tried new ways of meeting men, I learned how to improve my online dating techniques instead of giving up, blaming men, or shutting down.

And I got support. I hired a coach, I read books, I talked to friends. Just like I did to prepare for my TEDx speech. If the shy girl who moved past her paralyzing fear of public speaking can do a TEDx speech, you can move past your comfort zone when it comes to anything, especially dating.

I hope you'll be inspired to stretch yourself and do a few uncomfortable things in order to find love. It's so worth it!

Exercise On Saying YES!

- Make a list of five things you're avoiding that could help you grow and reach your potential.

- For the next five weeks, say YES to one of the things on your list. Figure out who you need to ask for help in order to make your YES happen. Journal about what happens

Step 26: Learn how to delegate

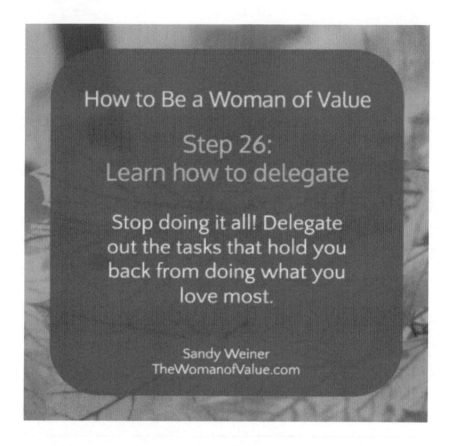

You don't get extra points for doing everything by yourself. You get drained. Learn how to delegate!

I am an independent strong woman. But, independence doesn't mean I want to live alone for the rest of my life, doing everything for myself. It doesn't mean I can't **"time-slot" a man into my life**, as some men have feared. Yes, my life is gloriously full, AND I want a relationship. Unfortunately, many of the men I date don't understand how that works.

A window into the life of an independent woman

I wasn't always a strong, independent woman. I've become self-reliant mostly by default. Before my divorce, I was more of a follower than a leader, more passive than active. Now, I'm an independent homeowner, bill payer, business owner, single mom, and CEO of my life. When I left my husband, I didn't realize how much responsibility I'd be taking on.

At times, it's overwhelming. I want to crawl under a rock and make all my responsibilities disappear. I want a knight in shining armor to come and whisk me away to an exotic island, sipping margaritas as we watch the sunset. But not for long, because I don't give up or give in easily. After all, I'm an independent woman. I enjoy the vibrant life I've created, but it's not yet complete.

I've earned my independence through sweat and tears

I've slain many dragons, most of them way before my divorce. Our firstborn child was born with many birth defects. In his first two years of life, he had 17 surgeries. We learned he had Fanconi Anemia, a rare genetic disease that often causes bone marrow failure and death, usually before a child reaches adulthood.

My husband was understandably overwhelmed and angered by our son's disease. When he shut down, I stepped up. I studied all the literature available at the library (there was no internet in those days). I became an expert in Fanconi Anemia, because most doctors had no idea what it was or how to treat it.

At the tender age of five, our sweet little boy died suddenly from a brain tumor. When my husband "disappeared" in his mourning, I became more independent, soldiering on to nurture our 3-year-old daughter and newborn son. It was lonely, losing my husband to his anger and depression after our son died.

I learned to do everything myself

I stopped asking for support because my husband was no longer capable of giving me what I needed. Like many women, I stayed married because I thought it was as good as it gets. When I looked at my friends' marriages, most of them weren't so different from mine. The wives were independently holding down the fort, and the husbands worked hard and were emotionally distant. Why leave my marriage if there was no better option? I thought it was crucial to give the kids a two-parent household, no matter what.

With therapy and increased self-awareness, I realized that I had been giving up too much of myself in this marriage. The cost was too high. There may not be Mecca out there on the other side of marriage, but I had to leave. I had to save myself. Divorce wasn't easy, but here I am, eight years later, living an incredibly rewarding life I'm proud to have created.

Many women become independent by default

What happened to me happened to a lot of women in dysfunctional marriages. When our husbands became emotionally distant, we took on more responsibility until we no longer asked for help. We become independent by default. We stopped asking for what we needed and wanted, because our past experiences told us we'd be ignored or worse, put down. So we learned to do it all. We stopped trusting that men would show up and be the loving partners we wanted and needed.

Taking responsibility for creating healthy relationships

Much of what happened in my marriage and in the marriages of other independent women boils down to two basic issues. One, we chose the wrong partners, men who shut us out when the going got tough and couldn't communicate well. Two, we had ineffective communication skills. Many women have trouble asking for what they want in an effective way.

Healthy mature relationships depend on the ability to choose a compatible partner, one with whom you feel safe enough to open up and be able to discuss anything, especially the hard stuff.

This independent woman doesn't want to be the sole proprietor of her life

I love running my own business as a dating coach, but I no longer want to do everything by myself. I have learned to ask for help in my professional and personal life. Most importantly, I want a good man in my life. No, I **need** a man—for intimacy, support, travel, and shared experiences of sorrow, joy, and appreciation for the simple pleasures of life.

The next time you put up that independent façade, know that deep inside, there probably lives a wounded little girl who sorely wants a relationship. Be more vulnerable, and open up to a potential partner. Don't be afraid to delegate and ask him for help.

You're looking for a strong man who will embrace your independence and give you permission to let go. Because you don't want to do it all by yourself anymore.

Exercise on Delegating

- Make a list of all the things you do that need to be done by you alone. These are in your zone of genius; writing, creating, leading.

- Now, make a list of all the tasks you don't have to do yourself. These include cleaning, cooking, running errands, shopping for food, and any administrative tasks that can be done by others.

- Take one item on your 'don't have to do yourself' list, and delegate it out to someone.

- Keep on doing this exercise until the only tasks you're doing are those that can only be done by you. Ahhhh. Doesn't that feel amazing?

Step 27: Be proactive, not reactive

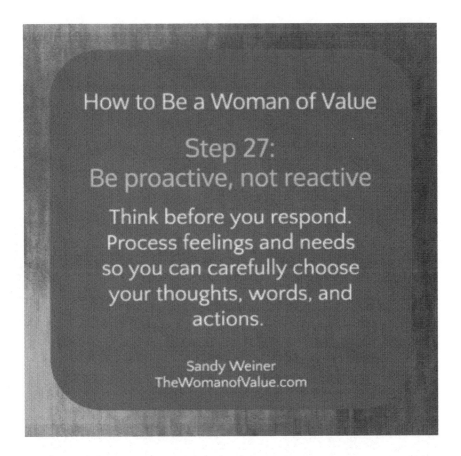

How to Be a Woman of Value

Step 27:
Be proactive, not reactive

Think before you respond.
Process feelings and needs
so you can carefully choose
your thoughts, words, and
actions.

Sandy Weiner
TheWomanofValue.com

Like many of you, I grew up in a home where there was a lot of arguing and yelling. Communication was often unclear and confusing. I do believe my parents were doing the best they could, but I was uncomfortable with the way they communicated. In spite of my awareness about what I didn't like about the culture of my home, I didn't have the skills to communicate effectively until my late 40s when I became a life coach and studied communication skills.

When I was married, I tried my best to not lose my cool when I was upset. I didn't yell very often, but my tone of voice reflected my anger. When my kids got older, they let me know how they felt. "Mom, watch your tone", they'd say. And that would make me even angrier. How dare they tell me what I'm doing wrong when I'm reprimanding them!

Now, I know better. And I'm grateful to my children for speaking up about how I came across when I was angry. I've learned to manage my tone, to think before reacting, and to process my emotions before speaking, especially when I need to have a tough conversation.

Following are ten steps for having a difficult conversation, especially with the man in your life.

Exercise: Being Proactive in Your Communication

1. **Process what you want to discuss.** Get clear about what happened and what you feel and need.

2. **Identify** whether it's your issue, his issue, or an issue that involved the two of you as a couple.

3. **Speak from a calm, open, vulnerable, soft, feminine space**, rather than a blaming, punishing, accusatory place. Be sure your tone is neutral. If not, give yourself empathy and take time to calm yourself down before talking.

4. **Check in and make sure it's a good time for him.** You can ask, "Is now a good time to talk?" If he says it's not, ask, "When would be a better time?" (Don't just walk away angry that he can't talk now. Men are usually single-task oriented, and if he's in the middle of something, he won't be able to focus until he's done.)

5. **Start with appreciation.** Appreciate him, his time, the relationship, the situation---whatever feels truthful to you.

6. **Acknowledge him and set him up to 'win':** Use words that will go right to his 'manly-heart' like save, help, hero, problem, solve, issue, solution, goal, result, provide, make possible, give, contribute, add, protect, etc.

7. **Make a clear/specific request:** It's helpful to add details, such as how long you've been experiencing the issue and the WHY of your request, complaint, or issue. If you're bringing up something you want to resolve, state the ultimate outcome, result, or goal you desire.

8. **Take responsibility for your role:** Ask if there's anything he needs from you in order to fulfill this request. You can ask, "Is there anything you need from me to do this?" or "Is there anything I'm missing that you think could be helpful?"

9. **Be prepared for a NO**: If he says no, there's usually a reason behind it. He believes he'll somehow "lose." 'NO' is often a code word for unarticulated fears. Once you know what they are, you can address them. You can ask, "Where do you think might you lose out if you did this for me?"

10. **End with Appreciation:** Express your appreciation for his *willingness* to fulfill your request, and express your appreciation again when he *fulfills* the request. A simple "thank you so much" is usually enough.

Practice having a difficult conversation with someone in your life.

If it's someone you're avoiding, that's even better! And if it doesn't go well the first few times, it's perfectly fine. It takes practice to improve your communication skills, one tough conversation at a time.

Step 28: Lean back

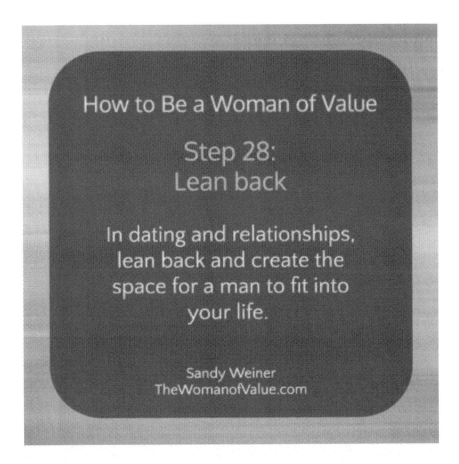

If you want to attract the type of man who inspires you, who shows up for you, and who consistently supports you, you must stop doing everything for him. LEAN BACK!

I received this letter from a woman who wanted to know why men disappear when she starts to show interest. Here's what I told her.

Hi Sandy,

I am 52 years young, in great shape for my age, and I seem to have no trouble attracting men. Here's my problem: I seem to keep attracting guys who fall head over heals for me almost immediately.

Then, one of two things happen. Either I become overwhelmed and put off by the intensity, and end the relationship after a date or two. Or, I become more attracted to them and start to reciprocate with affection and attention.

It seems that when I start to show interest, they pull away. I'm left scratching my head, trying to figure men out. Is it me or is it men, or is it a combination of the two? I don't want to play games, but I do want to be in a relationship with a good guy. Help!

Thanks,

Zara

Dear Zara,

You bring several issues, so allow me to outline what I think you're asking:

a) Why do you keep attracting men who attach and attract quickly?

b) Why do men pull away when you show interest?

c) Is it you or is it men?

Let's address each issue one at a time.

Why do you keep attracting men who attach and attract quickly?

Women who are confident, attractive, bright, and fun to be with tend to attract more men than others. You describe yourself as someone who attracts men easily. That's not your problem, so I hope you're grateful that you're way ahead of many women!

The problem is the guys who come on strong. I know the type well, because I tend to attract the same type of guy. They open up quickly. They let you know how attractive and sexy they think you are. They start communicating frequently via phone, text, email, video chat. They want to get together as quickly as possible.

What do you do when a guy comes on strong like that? Maybe you're turned on by his attention, especially if he's so open and forthcoming. It can be quite alluring. The problem is, it primarily feeds the ego, not your whole beautiful self. In other words, you can be swept away with the compliments and lose sight of what YOU want.

Pay attention to what happens to you when he compliments you and sweeps you off your feet.

Do you like HIM or do you like the compliments?

Proceed once you know where you're coming from. If you like him for all the right reasons, you can return his affection and know that the relationship might grow into something wonderful.

If you're attracted to the compliments, check in with your integrity and your heart. Ask yourself, "Do I really want to pursue this relationship?" Is there any substance beneath the 'love bombing' compliments and attention? If there is no depth beyond the flattering words, it might be time to let him go and seek out a relationship with someone with whom you can forge a healthy two-way bond, one where you're both attracted to each other for all the right reasons, not just to feed the ego.

Why do men pull away when you show interest?

A man who pursues you in this way can be a *hunter extraordinaire*. He's the guy who loves to hunt, to chase after his women. There is an adrenaline rush when he finally gets you. And then, the hunt is over and he's disinterested. He's onto the next woman.

Be very cautious of the hunter extraordinaire. He is not emotionally available for a relationship.

On the other hand, some guys like the chase, but they are also interested in a relationship. You might be coming on too strong when you respond to his attention.

Here's a typical scenario: Guy meets girl. Guy finds her really attractive. He tells her, "I think you're pretty and sexy." They talk on the phone. He texts her, "I like your voice." They speak again. He texts, "I think we have great chemistry." Makes you swoon a little. And makes you also wonder how real this is...

You're cautious but a little giggly. You feel desirable and sexy. You assume that all this talk means that he's interested in pursuing an exclusive relationship with you. So, you LEAN IN and escalate your efforts to get to know him. And he freaks out. Next thing you know, he's disappeared.

What happened? He didn't think you were in a relationship. He just finds you attractive. He chased after you because his 'small head' was attracted to you. His big head hadn't yet caught up.

With a guy like that, you need to LEAN BACK. Slow down. See if there is potential for a relationship. Women tend to think that flattery and pursuit = a possible relationship. Men don't usually feel the same way.

LEAN BACK. Don't shut down your online profile just yet. Don't stop dating other men. Keep your attitude breezy and light, and don't put any pressure on him to be in a relationship with you.

If you don't bring pressure to the relationship, he'll grow to love how he feels when he's with you. And ultimately, that's what he's looking for in a woman. Someone who makes him feel great.

Is it you or is it men?

I think it's a little of both. If you're putting the pressure on a guy by discussing 'where you are in your relationship' before there is one in his mind, that's something you can change.

You might be putting out a vibe that you don't need a man (but you want one to add to your already awesome life), which attracts men who like independent women. That's great, unless he's so independent, he's aloof and cold.

So, keep your intuition finely tuned and pay attention to these types of men when they show up in your life. Decide how you want to respond. Decide IF you want to respond at all.

Hey, there is probably a fantastic guy out there who falls for you right away because you are awesome. You don't want to reject him if he comes along.

Keep your head and heart balanced when meeting men. Make sure they know you are independent, but you also want a relationship and will make time for the right man.

Be a woman of value. Keep it real, keep your integrity, don't fall for potential, and have FUN! That should help you attract the right kind of man. Before you know it, you'll be going on your last first date.

Exercise: How to Lean Back When You're On a Date

Instead of filling every moment with conversation, ask a question and lean back. Stop talking. Wait for his answer, even if he doesn't speak for a minute or two.

When you're itching to take control and make the plans, pick the restaurant, or escalate the relationship, lean back. Tell a man what you want, what makes you happy, and see what he does. Give him the space to step up. You might be pleasantly surprised. And if he doesn't step up, you can step out before your heart is broken.

Step 29: Listen to understand

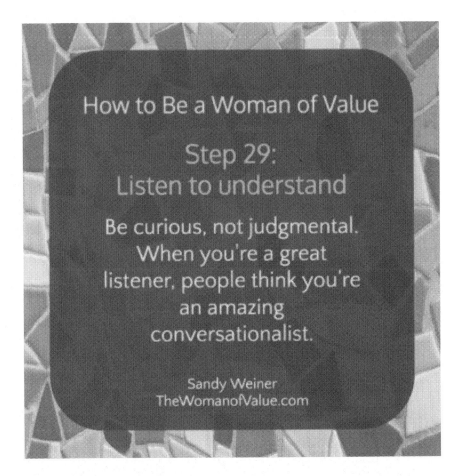

In Stephen R. Covey's wonderful book, The 7 Habits of Highly Effective People, principle number five is **Seek First to Understand, Then to be Understood.**

Most of us listen half-heartedly. We are usually forming our response while the other person is still talking, and we miss much of what is being said. What if we could all listen to understand?

This is important in all relationships, and it's especially important when women are talking to men. I love talking about how men and women can improve their communication, and that's why I hosted an interview with relationship coach, Ken Bechtel about the #1 key to being heard and understood by men.

Ken is an expert in the field of relationships and effective communication. He studied with **Alison Armstrong**, renowned expert on understanding men, so he knows his stuff!

Here are highlights of what we covered...

The #1 Key to Being Heard and Understood by Men

- **How to talk so he can hear you.** Ladies, men aren't ignoring you. They're single task focused, so you need to get their attention first. If they say they can't listen now, he's doing you a favor. Find out why.

- **The best ways to listen to the opposite sex.** Listen to understand. Stop talking. Create the space for a man to step up. Check in to be sure he's done speaking. Learn why you need to lean back, not lean in.

- **Why hinting doesn't work and never will.** Men will not pursue something that doesn't feel like it will work. It's also not an efficient use of their energy. Women love when a man gets the hint and buys them something or does something romantic. Find out why hinting backfires.

- **The difference between having needs and being needy.** It's important to express your own needs and feelings in a relationship. Needs are not needy, they are essential. What is needy? We reveal in the video.

- **How to get men to love listening to your detail laden stories.** Learn how to set a man up so he can hear your stories and track what you're trying to say, even if you're off topic!

- **The difference between compliments from men and women.** Women greet each other with compliments, validating, and it creates safety. Guys say, "Hey, asshole" to each other, because they don't have the need for connection to feel safe. When he compliments, he really means it. It's sincere. Accept it or he'll stop.

- **"I Do Not Think It Means What You Think It Means".** Words don't mean the same to both men and women. Learn what a man really means when he says, " I care for you".

You can watch the video on YouTube at https://youtu.be/yAbgiHaMydk.

Exercise: Your Takeaways From This Interview

- What are your key takeaways from my interview with Ken?

- Is there anything you'll do differently when speaking with men?

- If so, write about it in your journal.

- Practice your new understanding of men with every man you meet.

- Notice how men respond.

Step 30: If you want something, ask for it

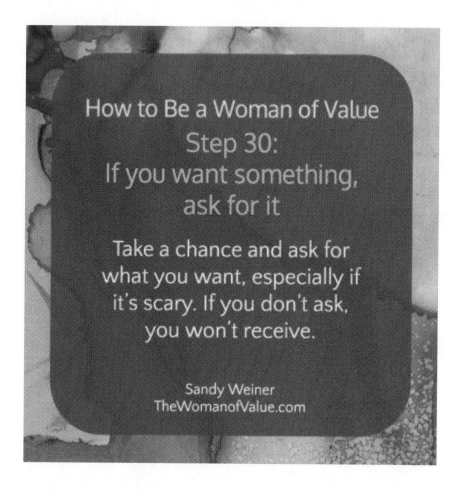

It took me a long time to learn the importance of asking for what I wanted in life and love. The problem with NOT asking for what you want is a) you receive what others think you want, b) you live a passive life, and c) you don't get what you want most of the time. That's no fun!

Why don't more people ask for what they want? Fear of rejection. Fear that you will sound demanding or entitled. It's all in HOW we ask and WHO we ask.

Let's apply this to your love life.

How often have your friends or family members offered to set you up on a blind date? Are you cringing at the mention of a set up? If you've ever been set up on a blind date, you know the results are often disastrous. I remember when I was in my twenties, I got set up quite often. Most of those dates were a total mismatch. I'd get upset with the person who introduced us as 'the perfect match for me'. "How could they have set me up with HIM? Do they even know me at all?"

Sound familiar? Setting up a friend on a blind date is a two-way street. And part of what makes a set up more successful is how proactive you are about ASKING FOR WHAT YOU WANT!

Let me explain...

How People Usually Ask for a Setup

1. Someone wants to introduce you to a potential date. Your friend or family member says they have the perfect person for you. What should you do or say? Ask lots of questions! Here are some examples: What about him makes him the perfect match for me? What can you tell me about his relationship history?

Ask about the core values that are important to you. If being family-oriented is important, ask what his relationship to his children or family of origin is like. If it's important that he's financially responsible, ask a question about his finances. Check him out before saying yes. One of the biggest problems in dating is wishful thinking. You create a fantasy of the man you're going to meet, and that almost always ends in disappointment. If you go in with your eyes closed, don't be surprised by what you find. If you do your homework, you will be able to assess the potentiality of the match before you go out. When setting up a friend on a blind date, **know before you go**. That's my motto.

2. The date didn't work out. What do you do or say? If you've properly vetted the guy before dating him, you've done your due diligence. You've been proactive, and you can't control the outcome, can you? So, the date wasn't the right fit for you. First, thank the person who set you up. Tell them that you appreciate the set up, and ask if they'd like feedback about the date. Start with the good. Providing specific feedback will give the person who set you up more clarity about what you are seeking in a potential match. Next time, they might be more on target with the setup.

3. If no one is setting you up, what can you do? How many times have you heard, "You're terrific. I wish I knew someone for you"? Set ups don't happen too often in the second half of life. The good news? You can do something about that! Here's something I did a few years back, and it yielded a few quality dates.

How to EFFECTIVELY Ask for a Setup

I copied my online dating profile to an email and sent it out to about 25 select friends, people whose social circles were different from mine. I added this cover letter:

Hi,

Hope you are well. As you may know, I have been dating for a few years since my divorce.

I have met some wonderful men and some not-so-wonderful men. I have dated men that I've met online and off-line, through set ups and through my own irresistible charms :)

Lately, I have found the dating scene to be quite frustrating. I want to get married again (and get it right this time).

As a dating coach, I advise my clients to try many avenues in order to find the right guy. So, I've decided to try something new. And for that, I need your help.

I am writing you because you are an important person in my life, and I believe you are connected to some awesome people.

You probably know many men that I don't know.

Would you be willing to think about any guy you might know, between the ages of 50 and 65, who might fit the type that I've outlined in my dating profile below?

I am not looking for a boy-meets-girl-because-they're-both-single kind of fix-up, but one where we're suited for each other, through commonalities and complements.

I have attached my full profile with the hope that it will give you a better idea about what kinds of things are important to me. I am hoping you might forward it to the right man.

Who knows? With your help, I am hoping to find Mr. Right.

One more thing: If you help me find him, you will be generously rewarded. The right man is worth his weight in gold to me.

Thank you for any help you may provide in helping me find love.

With love,

Sandy

Feel free to use my script, and personalize it so it sounds more like you. The important thing is that you need to ask for what you want. If you don't ask, and if you're not specific, how can you expect the results you are seeking? And don't forget to follow up a week or so later.

Exercise: Write to Ask For a Setup

Create your own letter asking friends/family for a setup. Send it out to 20 people, and follow up in a week. Watch what happens!

And remember, if someone is setting you up on a blind date, you need to check him out and ask questions. And don't get angry at your friends for setting you up with Mr. 'What-were-you-thinking?'. When you take responsibility for what you want, you'll have much better results.

Congratulations on making it to the end of the 30 steps!

I hope you continue to practice showing up, standing up, and speaking up. It's not enough to just read this book. Without implementation, whatever you read about how to become a woman of value will not be integrated into your being. That's why I urge you to do the exercises on a regular basis.

Your brain is amazingly flexible. When you create new habits, you change your brain. You create new neural pathways. That means, your brain processes in a healthier way. Over 90 days, those changes become permanent, and you will feel more confident...right down to your core.

- Sandy Weiner

About the Author

S andy Weiner guides women to show up more authentically, stand up and lead with grace, and speak up with confidence.

She's an internationally known TEDx speaker, women's empowerment coach, dating and relationship coach, author, podcast host, and retreat leader.

Sandy specializes in helping women achieve great things by overcoming fears, finding their authentic voice, and being valued for their full potential. She believes a **woman of value** is respected and rewarded for her contribution in life, work, and love.

To learn more about her work, visit her two websites:

https://lastfirstdate.com
https://thewomanofvalue.com

Made in the USA
Middletown, DE
24 May 2021